THE Possibilities OF PLAY

imaginative learning centers for children

Ages 3–6

Jean Feldman, PhD

Carolyn Kisloski

Gryphon House

www.gryphonhouse.com

Copyright

Bulk Purchase

Gryphon House books are available for special premiums and sales promotions as well as for fund-raising use. Special editions or book excerpts also can be created to specifications. For details, call 800.638.0928.

Disclaimer

Gryphon House, Inc., cannot be held responsible for damage, mishap, or injury incurred during the use of or because of activities in this book. Appropriate and reasonable caution and adult supervision of children involved in activities and corresponding to the age and capability of each child involved are recommended at all times. Do not leave children unattended at any time. Observe safety and caution at all times.

Table of Contents

Introduction · 1

Chapter 1: What Is Play? · 3

Chapter 2: Center Management · 11

Chapter 3: Small-Motor Center · 21

Chapter 4: Literacy Center · 43

Chapter 5: Writing Center · 65

Chapter 6: Math Center · 87

Chapter 7: Science Center · 109

Chapter 8: Block Center · 131

Chapter 9: Sensory Explorations Center· 151

Chapter 10: Dramatic Play Center · 159

Chapter 11: Art Center · 173

Chapter 12: Library Center · 191

Chapter 13: Listening and Technology Center· · · · · · · · · · · · · · · · · · 201

Chapter 14: Outdoor Adventures · 208

References and Recommended Reading · 224

Index · 228

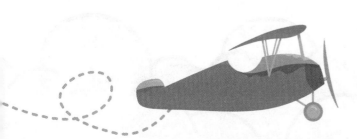

Introduction

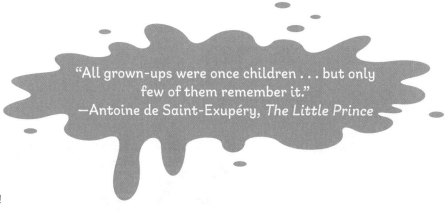

"All grown-ups were once children . . . but only few of them remember it."
—Antoine de Saint-Exupéry, *The Little Prince*

Let's play!

Learning centers are the most natural way to organize a classroom and encourage children to become active learners. Centers encourage children to make choices, explore at their own level, engage in hands-on discovery, solve problems, work with friends, use language, and be creative. Centers are also an effective way to use classroom materials, time, and space. Above all, learning centers capitalize on play, which is the most meaningful and fun way for children to learn.

Children's Bill of Rights to Play

The Declaration of Independence states that all Americans have the right to "Life, Liberty and the pursuit of Happiness." And that means children also have the right to play and live and learn in a way that makes them happy.

- Children have the right to enjoy life and play freely.
- Children have the right to believe that they are capable and worthy.
- Children have the right to hopes and dreams.
- Children have the right to wooden blocks and puzzles and playdough.
- Children have the right to swings and riding toys and sand boxes.
- Children have the right to hold hands with their friends and play games.
- Children have the right to play with toys.
- Children have the right to explore materials and make messes.
- Children have the right to play outdoors for long periods of time.
- Children have the right to use their imaginations and be creative.
- Children have the right to sing and dance and act silly.
- Children have the right to have books read to them—many, many books.
- Children have the right to smiles and hugs from adults who think they are the most wonderful children in the world.

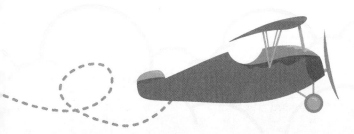

The more you know about the value of play, the more you can become an advocate for children and their right to play. *Play*. That beautiful little four-letter word that is at the heart of childhood. Play is the child's work, and play is how young children learn best. Friedrich Fröbel, inventor of kindergarten, had the right idea more than 150 years ago when he created "children's gardens."

How This Book Is Organized

This book will focus on the following centers: small-motor, literacy, writing, math, science, blocks, sensorimotor, dramatic play, art, library, listening, and technology, as well as activities for outdoor adventures. In each chapter, we offer an overview of how to create open-ended materials for the center, as well as specific activities that will engage children and nurture specific skills. Most of the ideas in this book are simple and inexpensive. You can make some of these center games and activities yourself, ask families to help you, or rotate shared materials with other teachers. We also offer ideas for setting up your centers, organizing how children use the centers, organizing your materials, and helping children learn how to use and return materials.

Before you can grow anything, you have to work long and hard to prepare the soil. Before children can grow into creative, well-adjusted, happy adults, we have to prepare the soil in their gardens. Singing, dancing, running outside, pretending, creating, building, laughing, exploring—these are the essential ingredients that will create the rich soil from which young children will grow.

What Is Play?

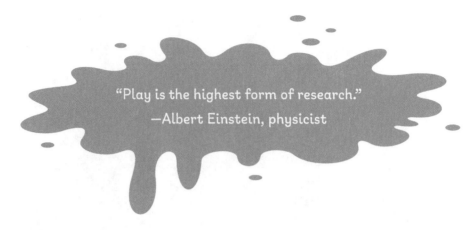

"Play is the highest form of research."
—Albert Einstein, physicist

Play: 1. noun. Activity engaged in for enjoyment and recreation, esp. by children.

2. verb. Engage in activity for enjoyment and recreation rather than a serious or practical purpose.

Stages and Types of Play

Play is natural and instinctive for all human beings. Researcher Mildred Parten (1932) identified six stages of play that children pass through as they develop and grow: unoccupied, solitary, onlooker, parallel, associative, and cooperative. Note that when children have mastered a stage of play, they will still return to it as they grow and develop. The age ranges listed are approximate; each child develops at his or her own pace (Rymanowicz, 2015).

· **Unoccupied play (birth to three months):** Babies observe the area around them or explore movements and materials with no organization as they begin to master their bodies.
· **Solitary play (birth to two years):** Children at this stage are busy exploring and discovering their world and are generally not interested in playing with other children.
· **Onlooker play (two years):** Children are interested in the play of other children, but they do not engage in that play. They learn about social rules and relationships by watching.
· **Parallel play (two to four years):** Children at this stage play next to each other because they are in the same area, but they don't interact.
· **Associative play (three to four years):** Children in this stage still play independently, but they begin to talk to other children, and borrow and take turns with toys.
· **Cooperative play (four years and up):** At this stage, children begin speaking, listening, communicating, and interacting with each other through play.

The ages and stages of the children you teach will significantly affect which materials and activities you choose. Within these stages of play are many different types of play. The National Institute for Play has identified these seven basic types.

- **Attunement**—This type establishes a connection, such as between a newborn and mother.
- **Body play and movement**—The infant explores the ways in which her body works and interacts with the world.
- **Object**—This type involves playing with toys and handling physical things out of curiosity.
- **Social**—This type of play involves another child or group of children.
- **Imaginative and pretend**—The child invents scenarios and acts within them.
- **Storytelling-narrative**—This is the play of learning and language, such as listening to a child retell a story.
- **Creative**—The child plays with imagination to transcend what is known to create a higher state.

All play is purposeful. There's not a rhyme, song, scribble, block structure, sandcastle, swing, laugh, dance, or hug that is wasted. It all integrates into the beautiful mosaic called childhood. In *free play*, children have the time, space, and materials to explore safely and engage with materials and peers in any way they choose. *Structured play*, in contrast, is often adult guided and supervised. There are rules and expectations and taking turns is involved. *Purposeful play* focuses on the learning opportunities that children develop as they engage in hands-on explorations. Purposeful play suggests taking skills children have to learn and turning them into something that they want to learn through games and engaging materials. Teachers add the magic to turn play into a learning adventure.

The Importance of Play

Play is disappearing. There are a multitude of social and cultural reasons for why children no longer have the freedom to play and to use their imaginations. Many researchers, including Joan Almon and Edward Miller, have addressed the issue. In their 2011 article "The Crisis in Early Education: A Research-Based Case for More Play and Less Pressure," Almon and Miller point out that no research supports the idea that children who read at age five do better in the long run than those who learn at six or seven; instead, they emphasize push-down academics at the cost of time for open-ended play negatively affects social-emotional development, curiosity, and language development. "Well-prepared early educators," Almon and Miller state, "need appropriate guidelines they can apply with flexibility."

Brain researchers, pediatricians, educators, child psychologists, and theorists agree that we must protect and preserve play. Study after study reports that children from play-based classes excel in reading, math,

and social and emotional adjustments (See, for example, Almon and Miller, 2011; Broadhead, Howard, and Wood, 2010; Nicolopoulou, 2010.) They also seemed to fare better as adults in work (Miller and Almon, 2009).

Social-Emotional Development

When children play in pairs or groups, they learn to share, communicate, empathize, cooperate, and collaborate. Play is essential for building relationships. Children can learn to solve their own problems through play. They learn to negotiate, listen, and compromise. In her book *Planning for Play: Strategies for Guiding Preschool Learning*, Kristen Kemple asserts that play not only helps children learn to negotiate conflicts in peaceful ways but also helps them learn to show awareness of others' rights, feelings, and well-being. Children learn to identify and name their own emotions and those of others when they play together (Kemple, 2017).

Play, especially vigorous outdoor play, is a great stress reliever and helps improve children's focus in the classroom (Taylor and Kuo, 2009; Kemple, 2017). Play develops executive function—understanding limits and being able to stop when necessary. Without play, there are more behavior problems in the classroom. Research supports the assertion that children with higher social and emotional competence will be more successful in school (Shonkoff and Phillips, 2000; Raver, 2002).

Play releases dopamine, a chemical that makes children feel happy and want to continue the play (Wang and Aamodt, 2012). Stuart Brown, founder of the National Institute for Play, put it this way in his 2008 TED Talk, "Play Is More Than Just Fun":

> The opposite of play is not work, it's depression. And I think if you think about life without play—no humor, no flirtation, no movies, no games, no fantasy, and, and, and. Try to imagine a culture or a life, adult or otherwise, without play. And the thing that's so unique about our species is that we're really designed to play through our whole lifetime.

Physical Development

In his book *Spark: The Revolutionary New Science of Exercise and the Brain* (2008), John Ratey argues that more physical fitness will lower obesity and improve academic performance. "Exercise stimulates the gray matter to produce Miracle-Gro for the brain . . . Dopamine, serotonin, and norepinephrine are elevated after exercise." These neurotransmitters can help with focus, calming down, and impulsivity.

Brown defines *body play*—jumping, rolling, swinging, running, climbing, and so on—as "a spontaneous desire to get ourselves out of gravity" (2008). When playing, children learn to experiment and take risks, which builds self-confidence. Children can develop self-help skills and independence, as well as large- and small-motor skills, when they play (Wang and Aamodt, 2012; Carlson, 2011). Play provides children with the opportunity to master their world and is closely linked with cognitive development.

Cognitive Development

Information gets to the brain through the senses. The more pathways you activate, the more likely the message will get to the brain and stay there. When children play, their whole brains are stimulated. Gwen Dewar, author of "The Cognitive Benefits of Play: Effects on the Learning Brain" (2014), reports the following:

- Play improves memory and stimulates the growth of the cerebral cortex.
- Play and exploration trigger the secretion of BDNF, a substance essential for the growth of brain cells.
- Children pay more attention to academic tasks when they are given frequent, brief opportunities for free play.
- There is a link between play and the development of oral language skills.
- Math skills benefit from play.

In 2001, researchers Charles Wolfgang, Laura Stannard, and Ithel Jones reported the results of a long-term study that began in 1982. Beginning with a group of children who were four years old, the researchers studied the complexity of the children's block play and then they followed their math skills through high school. Wolfgang, Stannard, and Jones found a positive relationship between the complexity of the children's block play and their later math ability in high school. Dewar describes the results this way: "Of course, these results might merely tell us that kids who are smart in preschool continue to be smart in high school. But it's not that simple. The association between block play and math performance remained even after researchers controlled for a child's IQ. It therefore seems plausible that block play itself influenced the cognitive development of these kids."

In their clinical report for the American Academy of Pediatrics, researcher Kenneth Ginsburg and colleagues note: "Studies have found that children who engage in dramatic games of make-believe develop stronger language skills, better social skills, and more imagination than children who do not play this way" (2011). As children interact, test their physical abilities, and work together to create play scenarios, they learn skills such as task initiation, joining in play, and making play suggestions (Kemple, 2017; Kostelnik et al., 2014; National Council for the Social Studies, 2010).

Play develops oral language skills and vocabulary as well as math skills (see Weisberg et al., 2015; Sutherland and Friedman, 2013; Zigler, Singer, and Bishop-Josef, 2004; Ginsberg and Seo, 2009; Fisher et al., 2013; Levine et al., 2011). For example, researcher Kelly Fisher and colleagues found that children who were taught

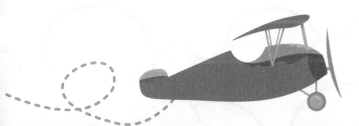

shapes within a context of guided play showed better shape knowledge than children who were taught shapes through direct teaching (for example, "This is a square. It has four sides."). Kemple describes an example of guided play in her book *Planning for Play*. The teacher wants to support children's understanding of putting shapes together to make other shapes. In the block center, she watches as two children build a wall:

> When the 1-unit blocks have run out and there is still a section of wall remaining to complete, Nick picks up two right-triangle blocks and tries to set them together on the wall to substitute for a 1-unit block, but they slide apart. [His teacher] offer[s] Nick some masking tape to stick the two triangle blocks together: "Will this help?"

> This serves to consolidate his understanding that two right-triangle blocks can be put together to make a square.

In her book *Play Today: Building the Young Brain through Creative Expression*, author Ann Barbour asserts that language is a natural part of dramatic play. Children use language to plan, organize, and structure their play. They use situation-specific language to support the roles they are playing.

Children tell us things through their play because it serves as a bridge between fantasy and reality. Play nurtures children's individual talents and interests as children follow their ideas and imagine scenarios with peers. Children can express new insights and be creative through play, taking on roles and imagining new functions for familiar objects (Bodrova, Germeroth, and Leong, 2013). Through imagining, planning, testing, and making decisions, children build their abilities to respond to change creatively (Brown, 2008).

Play also provides opportunities to support emerging literacy skills. Barbour points out that children typically start out in dramatic play imitating tasks or skills they have seen in everyday life, such as cooking. Gradually, their play will develop into a story-type narrative, with a beginning, a middle, and an end. Teachers can support children's understanding of literacy skills by providing paper and writing utensils, such as an order pad and pen for the "restaurant" or paper, envelopes, and markers for the "post office." Menus, empty food containers, and other items with words on them can also support children's skills at recognizing letters and even some words.

Play Benefits the Whole Child

Every child deserves time to play, space to play, open-ended materials to explore, and friends to play with. Through play the whole child is nurtured—intellectually, physically, socially, and emotionally. Play can build childhood memories of joy, delight, friendship, confidence, and hope that will serve them well as they travel through their lives.

Our goal is to share learning activities in which children will naturally learn as they play. Let's take skills that children need to learn and turn them into something that they *want* to learn, with challenging, hands-on, playful centers.

Even though children learn through play, they also need opportunities that challenge them to think, explore, and master new skills and concepts. Balance is the key to successful learning for all students, and that is why you will find a broad range of learning activities in this book. Children need opportunities to work with a small group, and they need materials that will help them learn independently and want to repeat activities. They need choices so they can be creative with open-ended activities, but they also need centers where there are specific tasks that focus on skills.

Preschool, prekindergarten, and kindergarten teachers will find lists of materials that will appeal to a wide range of learning interests and abilities. Most of the materials used are common classroom objects and natural items that are easy to prepare. Many objects are recycled or inexpensive. The directions are clear and simple to follow, and the photographs provide good visual examples.

Intentional teaching suggests that there is a reason and purpose for each center. The activities in this book can easily be modified for specific age levels and skills. We explain the goals and skills that children can develop as they interact in each center; however, it's important to remember that there are always multiple ways that children can grow academically, socially, and emotionally.

In addition to indoor activities, we offer ideas for providing centers and learning experiences outside on the playground. When children are outdoors, they feel freer to explore, laugh, and make a mess.

Nothing succeeds like success. When children have fun and are successful learning in centers, they will be motivated to learn more. They will feel confident in their abilities and be excited about new challenges.

Families often want to know what their children are "learning" at school. Here is a poem to share with families to remind them how children learn through play.

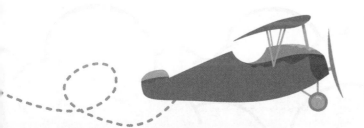

What's in Your Backpack?

By Dr. Jean

What's in your backpack?
It's empty today.
Where's your work?
Did you just play?

When I built with blocks
I learned about shapes.
I balanced and shared—
Our skyscraper was great.

I played in the windy house
And talked with my friends.
I rocked a baby
And played pretend.

In science I observed,
Guessed, and experimented, too.
The same things grown-up
Scientists do.

Art was messy.
I created and explored.
I solved my own problem
When I spilled glue on the floor.

My fingers got a workout
With puzzles and clay.
Those same muscles
Will help me write one day.

I counted and sorted
And measured, too.
I used my brain
Like a math whiz would do.

Out on the playground
I ran like the wind.
I learned to take turns
And helped a hurt friend.

Story time is what
I always like best.
I can use my imagination
And give my body a rest.

I sang and danced,
Learned a finger play, too.
I answered questions
And said "please" and "thank you."

There will be time
For worksheets and tests,
But talking and playing
Is how I learn best.

I love to go to school.
I'm glad I'm me.
An empty backpack
Means I'm learning, you see.

The Possibilities of Play

Center
Management

"Play is the work of the child."
—Maria Montessori, founder of the Montessori method of education

In this book, we refer to a *learning center* as a designated area in the classroom with interesting materials where children can explore, practice, and be active learners. Children need a variety of learning experiences in their school day—large group, small group, and independent. Learning centers provide balance by allowing children to make choices and learn in their own special ways.

- Hands-on activities in centers provide many pathways to the brain and are engaging for young learners.
- In centers, each child can work at his own pace and level.
- Centers offer children opportunities to develop executive function skills, such as task initiation and task completion.
- Centers enhance twenty-first-century skills as children cooperate with others, communicate, solve problems, and think critically.
- Centers give children the opportunity to develop organizational skills and responsibility.
- Centers can provide children with purposeful practice as they begin to develop automaticity*.
- Centers give children a meaningful foundation from which they can continue to grow.

*Researchers Pamela Hook and Sandra Jones define *automaticity* as "the fast, accurate, and effortless" ability to identify words. It can also be used in reference to the ability to quickly identify numbers and shapes, among other skills. That does not mean, however, that drills, worksheets, and endless repetition are developmentally appropriate for young children. Children learn through play!

The teacher's role is that of a facilitator. Provide children with challenges, opportunities to learn, and open-ended materials, and then trust them to construct their own knowledge in their own unique ways. Sometimes you will want to create open centers where children can freely explore and do what they want. Other times you will want to have specific tasks for the children to complete. Balance open-ended explorations with skill-based centers where children can learn, repeat experiences, and talk about what they are doing with classmates. Children will understand that they must complete their "have to" activities before they can choose a "want to" activity. That's why it's important to have several choices in each center with "want to" materials. Model, model, model—thoroughly explain each center, and demonstrate how to use the materials and clean up so the children are clear about what you expect.

Tips for Center Success

Children need large blocks of time to work in centers. Most experts recommend forty-five minutes to an hour, to give children enough time to develop their play ideas and explore thoroughly. Limit the number of children who can be in a center at one time, so they will have ample materials and space to explore.

Carefully select materials and equipment to meet your goals and the developmental needs of the children. Provide and change centers and materials based on your students' interests, needs, and your curriculum goals. Not all centers have to be set up in your classroom at the same time, nor do they each need to be on one skill or subject. You might integrate math and science or writing and the computer, for instance. Avoid clutter in centers by rotating the materials, and introduce materials slowly so children aren't overwhelmed by too many choices.

Arrange centers according to noise level and activity type. For example, quieter centers, such as the library and reading area, should be grouped together. Add a rug to the library for warmth and comfort. Noisier or messier centers, such as blocks and art, should be set up away from quiet spaces. Art and sensory play should be on washable flooring near a sink, while blocks should be on carpeting to keep down the noise. Partition the room with shelves, bookcases, and dividers to create smaller spaces where children can concentrate and not get distracted.

Center Management

There are many ways to make chocolate chip cookies, but they all taste yummy. Similarly, there are many ways to manage centers, but you've got to make them fun and yummy for the children. Some teachers swear by a choice board. Others prefer task cards or tickets. Your curriculum, schedule, goals, and the children you teach will influence your choice of strategies. The best one is the one that works best for you.

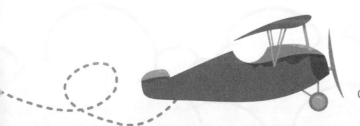

Choice Board

Make a choice board on a piece of poster board, using photos of the different learning centers you have in your classroom. Put dots next to each photo to represent the number of children who can play in each center at a given time. Write each child's name on a clothespin, and keep them in a cup or basket by the choice board. When it's time for centers, pass out the clothespins (or assign that task to a classroom helper). Children can clip their clothespins by the centers where they would like to play. If all the spaces (dots) are used, then they must make another choice. To make the process go more smoothly, use alphabetical order to determine who chooses first each day. For example, on Mondays, the first five children in the alphabet get first choice. On Tuesdays, the next five in the alphabet get to choose, and so on. In this way, each child will get her first choice one day and be last to choose another day. Children may stay in their chosen centers as long as they want. When a child is ready to move to another center, he can remove his clothespin and attach it next to the photo of another center that is open.

The best strategy for center management is the one that works best for you and the children you teach.

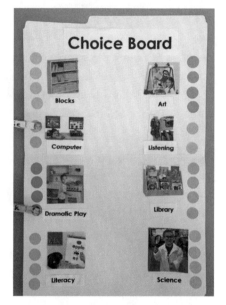

Checklist

Put a checklist with children's names on it in each center. As each child completes the activity in the center, she can mark her name off the list and write a "comment," such as a smiley face or a frown.

Task Cards

Create a task card for each child to complete at centers during the week. For example, on an index card, draw a grid with eight to ten spaces. Write the name of each center and put pictures or drawings of the activities or materials available in each center. You can make a master copy of the card and reproduce blank copies each week. As each child completes a center, have her color in the icon. Children may choose the order in which they do the activities and may stay as long as they want at each center. Hint: As children complete activities, have them

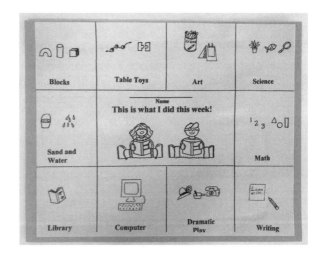

raise their hands so that you can punch holes in their cards and ask about what they did. If they complete all designated tasks by the end of the week, then they earn Fabulous Friday time (free time to play in centers).

Journals

Pass a play phone around, and ask children to state which center they'd like to work in and what they would like to do there. Alternatively, pass out the children's journals and ask them to write or draw which center they would like to work in and what they plan to do there. At the end of center time, have them draw pictures or dictate sentences in their journals about what they did and learned.

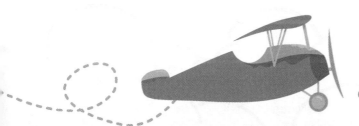

Tickets to Centers

Cut out pictures that represent the different centers in your classroom. Cut out a number of pictures for each area that equals the number of children who can play in that area. Glue the pictures to poster board cut into 4-inch squares to create tickets. At center time, shuffle the tickets and allow each child to draw one. Children then go to the centers shown on their tickets.

Pick Three

Write the children's names down the left side of a sheet of poster board. Attach three small adhesive hooks beside each child's name. Cut out 3-inch circles, laminate them if possible, and punch a hole in the top of each one. Write the name of a different classroom center on each circle. Each day, hang three different center circles beside each child's name for her to complete that day. Children should do the assigned centers in sequence, and then they may have free choice.

Clothespins, Bracelets, and Badges

Use colored bracelets, clothespins, or badges to limit the number of children who can play in each center. To help with organization, color-code the clothespins, bracelets, or badges and the labels for the corresponding center materials. For example, the dramatic play/housekeeping center could be orange; the blocks area could be brown; the art center could be purple, and so on.

By the center entrance, place the number of clothespins, bracelets, or badges representing the number of children allowed in that center at one time. For example, you might have four clothespins clipped to the sign for the block center or six badges in a basket by the dramatic play center. Each child who wants to play in that center should attach a clothespin to his clothing (or put on a bracelet or badge) and wear it while he plays in the center. When he decides to move to another center, he should remove the clothespin, bracelet, or badge and put it back so that another child can take his place. If there aren't any clothespins available when a child wants to play in the center, he must wait until a child in that center puts her clothespin back on the sign or returns her bracelet or badge to the basket.

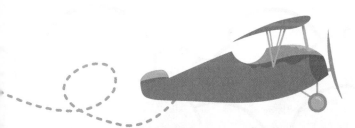

Center Rotation

Center rotation is another option if you want all children to work in small groups and experience different centers and activities. Each day you will have the opportunity to work with a small group, and then they can rotate through three different centers.

Number four pieces of paper, and then tape each number to a center you would like the children to visit. Number 1 will always be the teacher-directed activity. Number 2 could be an open-ended play center, such as blocks or housekeeping. Number 3 could be an art activity, writing, or a small-motor task. Number 4 could be the listening and the technology center, the library, or the math center. You can vary which centers you use according to the children's abilities at different times of the year and what your goals are.

Next, number small pieces of paper, one number per paper, and put them in a basket. You will need as many pieces of paper as there are children in your room. Allow each child to choose a number and begin his rotation at the corresponding center. After 15–20 minutes, have children clean up the centers they are in and rotate in a clockwise direction to the next center. For example, children in station one go to two, in two go to three, in three go to four, and in four go to one. Within an hour or so, children will have had the opportunity to experience four different activities, including working with the teacher.

Tips to help center rotation work smoothly:

- You can either create four groups based on skill levels or randomly assign children to different stations where they should start.
- Use a timer to make sure everyone gets the same amount of time in an area.
- Adapt the length of time to the ages and abilities of your students.
- Exercise or do a brain break between rotations.
- Have several choices in each station. After children complete the "main course"—the assigned task—they can have "dessert" or free choice.

- **Teacher-directed activities**
  - » Phonological awareness
  - » Reading readiness
- **Social play**
  - » Housekeeping
  - » Blocks

- **Small-motor skills**
  - » Puzzles
  - » Playdough
  - » Dry-erase boards/ chalkboard
  - » Art
  - » Blank books

- **Independent exploration**
  - » Listening center
  - » Library
  - » Math
  - » Technology
  - » Science

Materials Management

Store center materials in ziplock bags, pencil boxes, baskets, or clear plastic tubs. Label each container with both the words for and a picture of the materials that belong in it. Labeling toys and games will help children know where to store items when they are finished. Model how to care for the materials in the centers, complete an activity, and clean up.

To create simple picture labels for your containers, you will need two pictures for each toy in your classroom and some clear contact paper or clear packing tape. Print two pictures of each toy in your classroom. Adhere one picture to the bin that holds the toy, using clear contact paper or clear packing tape. Adhere the other picture to the location where you would like students to return the toy.

At the beginning of the year, explain that everything in the classroom has a place. Each place is labeled so students can easily find where each toy belongs. To help the children practice putting materials where they belong, show them a box labeled *pencils* that is full of pencils; a box labeled *crackers* full of crackers, and a bin labeled *Legos* full of Legos plus some housekeeping food. Explain to the children that when you open a labeled package, you expect to find what is on the label inside the package. Open each bin in turn, read the label, and show the children the photo on the label, then show them the materials inside the bin. When you open the Lego bin, express shock at finding play food inside, because that is not what the label said would be in there. Ask the children where the play food should be. Each day after cleanup, continue to demonstrate how the correct items should be in the correct bins and give the children plenty of practice so they learn to put items back where they belong.

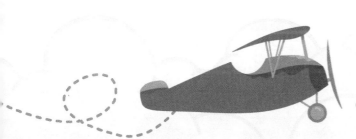

Small-Motor Center

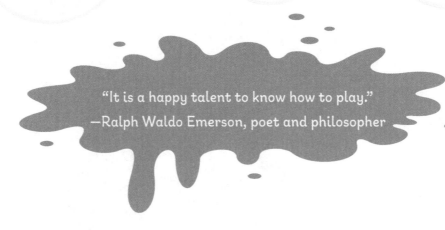

"It is a happy talent to know how to play."
—Ralph Waldo Emerson, poet and philosopher

As children play with table toys, they learn how to begin and complete tasks. They develop their small muscles, eye-hand coordination, attention span, social skills, and language skills. They also build concepts about size, shape, color, and patterns. Activities in the small-motor center are like sending those little fingers to the gym!

Research tells us that small-motor skills, along with attention and general knowledge, are much stronger predictors of later math, science, and reading scores than early math and reading scores alone (Grissmer et al., 2010). So, give the children plenty of opportunities to playfully develop these skills.

Materials for the Small-Motor Center

Table and chairs	Nuts and bolts	Lacing activities	Parquetry blocks
Puzzles	Child-safe scissors	Nesting toys	Paper and pencils
Beads		Locks and keys	Clay
Sewing cards	Pattern cards	Take-apart toys	Board games
Pegboard	Playing cards	Hole punches	Snap toys
Dressing toys	Puzzle rack	Playdough and tools	

Tip: Encourage the children to wash their hands before and after using small-motor materials.

The Possibilities of Play

Tearing Tub

Learning Opportunities

Small-motor skills
Creativity
Eye-hand coordination
Social skills

Materials

Plastic tub
Tissue paper
Wrapping paper
Construction paper
Scrap paper

What to Do

Place various types of paper in the tub, and encourage the children to tear the paper and make confetti. For a fun variation, you can take this activity outside, where you let the children gather leaves, pine straw, and other natural materials they find on the playground. Encourage them to tear the materials into pieces. Explain how natural materials will decompose and turn into soil. If you have a compost bin, let the children add their natural items to it when they are finished exploring. Or, encourage them to use the confetti and natural items to create collages.

Cutting Pool

Learning Opportunities

Small-motor skills
Bilateral coordination
Oral language
Social skills
Independence

Materials

Small plastic swimming pool
Junk mail
Paper scraps
Catalogs
Child-safe scissors

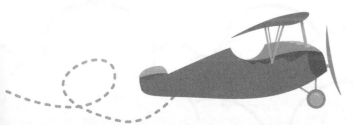

What to Do

This activity is great for indoor or outdoor play. Put different types of paper scraps in the pool. Provide child-safe scissors, and invite the children to get in the pool and cut, cut, cut. For even more fun, provide decorative scissors that make patterns like waves or zig-zags when they cut.

Hole-Punch Box

Learning Opportunities

Small-muscle strength
Eye-hand coordination
Spatial awareness

Materials

Hole punches, 1 per child
Paper
Index cards
Paper plates
Shoeboxes
Plastic bottles with lids
Jingle bells

What to Do

Put hole punches on a picnic table on the playground.

Children can hole punch designs in the paper, paper plates, index cards, or shoeboxes, which will strengthen their small muscles.

For even more fun, punch little holes in plastic bottles and add jingle bells to make shakers.

Lids

Learning Opportunities

Eye-hand coordination
Spatial awareness
Small-muscle strength
Independence

What to Do

Put a little toy in each jar and then screw on the lid.
Children get to open the jars and take out the toys,
which will be like opening presents to them. When
they've removed all the toys, they can put them
back in the jars and screw the lids back on. Take the
fun outside to the sandbox or to a water table on the
playground.

Materials

Plastic jars with lids, in a variety of sizes
Small toys and other interesting objects

String-Along Tub

Learning Opportunities

Eye-hand coordination
Task initiation and
completion
Creativity

Materials

Plastic tub
Beads
Paper straws
Large buttons
Chenille stems, yarn,
or string
Masking tape

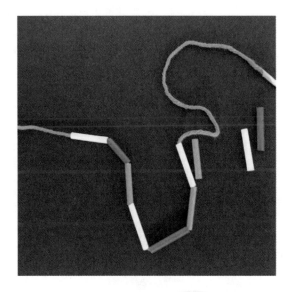

What to Do

Cut the straws into short pieces. Add them and the
other items to the tub. Encourage the children to
string items from the tub onto the chenille stems to
make bracelets.

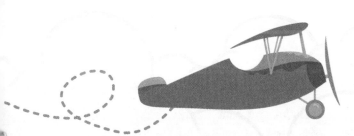

If you are using yarn or string, knot one end and wrap masking tape around the other end to make it easier to string items.

For more fun and creativity, let the children gather natural items such as leaves and flowers to string on their bracelets.

Clothespins and Tongs

Learning Opportunities

Eye-hand coordination
Small-motor skills
Self-help skills

Materials

Bowl or bucket
Spring-type clothespins
Tongs
Chopsticks
Pompoms
Cotton balls
Other small items

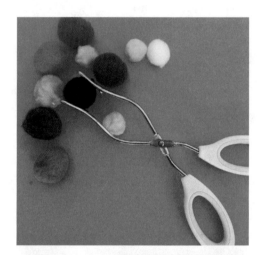

What to Do

Set out the clothespins or tongs, along with pompoms, cotton balls, and other small items. Place the bowl alongside these items. Encourage the children to use a clothespin or tongs to pick up the items and put them in a bowl. For even more challenge, encourage the children to transfer small objects from one place to another using chopsticks.

Outside, encourage the children to use tongs to collect nuts, rocks, and other natural items and put them in a bucket.

Poke Designs

Learning Opportunities

Small-motor skills
Identifying shapes
Identifying letters
Task initiation and completion

Materials

Construction paper
Marker
Traceable letters or shapes
Mouse pad or carpet sample
Toothpick or pencil

What to Do

Use the marker to trace letters or shapes on the construction paper.

Place the paper on top of a mouse pad or carpet sample, and encourage the children to poke around the design outlines with a toothpick or pencil, and then hold the paper up to the light. They will be able to see the light coming through the outlines. Talk with the children about the shapes or letters they are working with.

For more fun, the children can do these on the ground outdoors and then hold the papers up to let the sunshine reveal their letters or shapes.

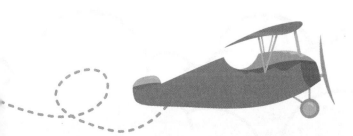

Puzzles

Learning Opportunities

Small-motor skills
Task initiation and completion
Using recyclable materials

Materials

Empty cereal and food boxes
Scissors
Legal-sized clasp envelopes or ziplock bags

What to Do

Cut off the front cover of each box and cut it into puzzle shapes. Vary the number of puzzle pieces according to the abilities of the children. Make two- or three-piece puzzles for younger children and puzzles with more pieces for older children.

Store the different puzzles in envelopes or ziplock bags.

Hint: It works well to have two boxes of the same type. Cut one up to make a puzzle, and then the children can match the pieces to the uncut box.

Stencils

Learning Opportunities

Prewriting skills
Small-motor skills
Using recyclable materials
Eye-hand coordination

Materials

Empty food boxes
Pencils
Colored pencils
Scissors
Paper

What to Do

Cut shapes out of food boxes. You might cut geometric shapes, holiday and seasonal shapes, or animal shapes. Encourage the children to trace around the shapes on paper with colored pencils.

Outside, put out paper and pencils on a picnic table, and encourage the children to find objects on the playground that they can trace around.

For even more fun, children can trace around puzzle pieces, cookie cutters, jar lids, and other classroom objects.

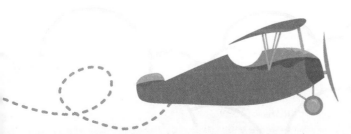

Sewing Cards

Learning Opportunities

Eye-hand coordination
Using recyclable materials
Small-motor skills

Materials

Fronts from food boxes
Colorful paper plates
Greeting cards
Hole punch
Shoelaces or cord

What to Do

Punch holes around the edges of the fronts of food boxes, paper plates, and cards. Children can sew through the holes with shoelaces or cord.

For a quiet activity outside, perhaps for the children to do while you are reading a story to them, take sewing cards and shoelaces or cord out to the playground.

Inserting

Learning Opportunities

Eye-hand coordination
Spatial awareness
Small-motor skills

Materials

Clean, empty potato-chip canister with lid
Scissors
Poker chips
Plastic bottles and containers
Small rocks or sticks

What to Do

Cut a slit in the lid of a potato-chip canister to make a bank. Give the children poker chips, and ask them to put them in the bank.

Outside, invite the children to insert small rocks or sticks in plastic bottles and containers. Can they take them out?

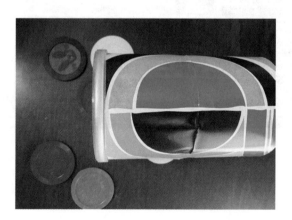

Baby Dolls

Learning Opportunities

Self-help skills
Small-motor skills
Self-confidence
Independence

Materials

Baby dolls
Doll clothes with snaps, zippers, and buttons
Wagon or pull toy
Plastic tub
Water
Soap

What to Do

Invite the children to dress and undress the dolls.

As you prepare to go outside, ask the children to dress the dolls for outdoor play. What do they need to wear if it's cold outside? Let children give the dolls a ride in a wagon or pull toy. On a warm day, let children wash the dolls and doll clothes in a tub of soapy water.

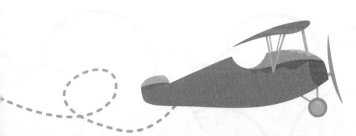

> ### Playdough
>
> Playdough is multisensory, engaging, creative, and open ended. It's great to just put out playdough and let children create whatever they want, but playdough can also be a teaching tool. Using playdough activities is a natural and meaningful way for children to learn as they play, have fun, and interact with their friends.

Playdough Center

Learning Opportunities

Creativity

Problem solving

Small-motor skills

Imagination

Independence

Self-expression

Stress relief

Social skills

Materials

Playdough

Craft sticks, toothpicks, straws, chenille stems

Plastic utensils (knives, forks, spoons)

Cupcake papers, birthday candles

Buttons, googly eyes

Rolling pin (or cylinder block)

Natural items (shells, sticks, leaves, feathers)

Cookie cutters, child-safe scissors

Small toy animals

Seasonal or holiday objects

Hints and Suggestions

- To keep the children's interest, vary the items in the center, introducing one or two at a time.
- Lunchroom trays, cookie sheets, or plastic mats will help keep playdough in a defined space.
- Have simple rules. For example:
  - » Keep the playdough in your space.
  - » Share the materials.
  - » Clean up when you are finished.
  - » Use one color at a time.
- Children should wash their hands before and after using playdough.

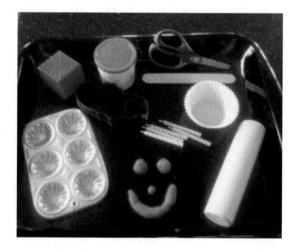

- Beware of allergies, and offer gluten-free playdough and fragrance-free playdough when needed. (You can find recipes using rice flour online.)
- Some classrooms like to provide individual containers of playdough for each child. Parent volunteers can make a new batch of playdough each month and make personal bags for the children.

Homemade Playdough

You can purchase playdough or use one of these recipes to make your own.

2 cups all-purpose flour
1 cup salt
2 Tbsp. cream of tartar
2 Tbsp. vegetable oil
2 cups water
food coloring

Mix together the food coloring and water. Add the colored water and the rest of the ingredients to a pot, and stir until smooth. Cook over medium heat, stirring constantly until the mixture forms a ball and sticks to the spoon. Cool and knead. Add more food coloring, if desired. Store in plastic bags or covered containers.

Variations

- Add oil of mint or other extracts* to playdough to give it a fragrance.
- Use 2 Tbsp. baby oil or massage oil in place of the vegetable oil.
- Unsweetened, fruity drink mix can be used in lieu of food coloring. The drink mix will add a sweet aroma.
- For gluten-free playdough, substitute rice flour for wheat flour.

> *Safety Note: Check for allergies or sensitivities before using extracts or wheat products with children.

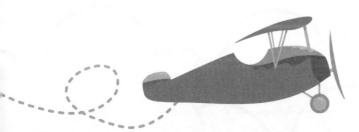

Biscuit-Mix Playdough

2 cups commercial biscuit mix, such as Bisquick
1 cup salt
2 cups water
1 Tbsp. cream of tartar
1 Tbsp. vegetable oil

Mix all ingredients in a microwave-safe bowl. Microwave for 3 minutes on high. Scrape and stir the bowl. Microwave for another 3 minutes, then stir. If it's not quite ready, then microwave for another minute and stir. Cool and knead.

Literacy Skills

Letter Plates

Learning Opportunities

Alphabet knowledge
Small-motor skills
Task initiation and completion

Materials

Clear plastic plates
Permanent marker
Playdough

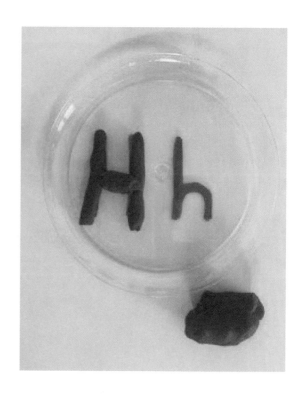

What to Do

Write letters on clear plastic plates with a permanent marker. Invite the children to roll playdough and place it on the plates in the shapes of the letters. Encourage them to make something out of playdough that begins with the letter sounds.

Playdough Stories

Learning Opportunities

Story comprehension
Small-motor skills
Oral language skills
Sequencing

Materials

Playdough

What to Do

Encourage the children to make their favorite characters out of playdough. Then they can use their figurines to retell a story.

For even more fun, after reading a nonfiction book to them, encourage the children to make something that they learned about from the book.

Playdough Writing

Learning Opportunities

Letter recognition skills
Emerging literacy skills
Small-motor skills

Materials

Playdough
Golf tees

What to Do

Encourage the children to use golf tees to practice making letters and writing words in playdough.

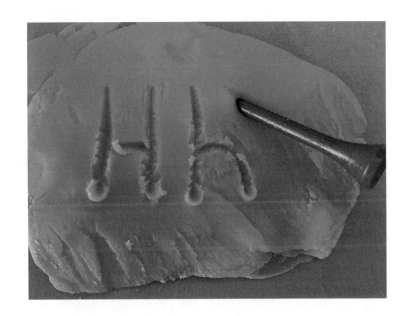

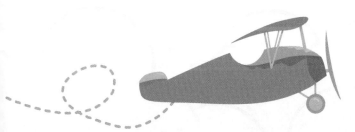

Playdough Sight Words

Learning Opportunities

Emerging literacy skills
Small-motor skills
Oral language skills
Letter recognition skills

Materials

Playdough
Card stock or paper
Marker
Clear sheet protectors

What to Do

Write sight words in a bubble font on pieces of paper or card stock. Place each paper in a clear sheet protector. Invite the children to roll playdough into the shapes of the letters on top of the words. For a bigger challenge, encourage them to write the words.

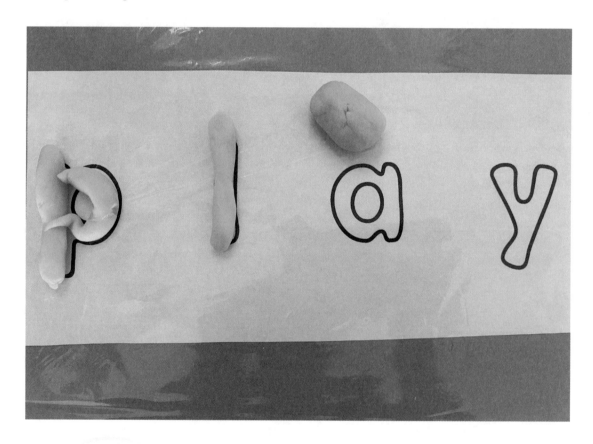

STEM Learning

Playdough Book

Learning Opportunities

Small-motor skills
Eye-hand coordination
Geometric shapes
Task initiation and completion

Materials

4 file folders
Construction paper
Markers
Glue
Book rings
Clear contact paper

What to Do

Gather four file folders. Turn each folder vertically, with the fold on the left-hand side. Punch two holes along the left side of each folder at the fold.

Open the first folder. Inside, write, "Can you make lines?" Draw some straight lines on the inside of the folder.

Open the next folder and write, "Can you make curves?" Draw some curves on the folder.

Inside the third folder, write, "Can you make shapes?" Draw a square, rectangle, circle, triangle, and so on.

Inside the fourth folder, write, "What else can you make?" Draw simple objects, such as a nest and eggs, hot dogs, a bunny, and so on.

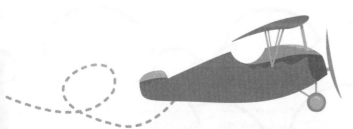

Stack the folders, and bind them together with book rings. Make a cover for the book by creating a label from construction paper to glue to the top of the first folder. For added durability, cover the pages with clear contact paper.

Show the children the book and read each page to them. Challenge the children to roll playdough and place it on top of the lines and shapes.

One-to-One Correspondence Mats

Learning Opportunities

One-to-one correspondence
Number recognition
Small-motor skills

Materials

Playdough mats or paper
Markers
Clear sheet protectors
Playdough

What to Do

Download printable playdough mats free from the internet, or create your own. Use a counting fingerplay, such as "Five Little Hot Dogs Frying in the Pan," or a unit of study, such as flowers and stems in the springtime, as your theme. Slide the mats into clear sheet protectors.

Encourage the children to roll the playdough to match with the pictures on the mats. Count the number of items as the children match the pictures.

Number Mats

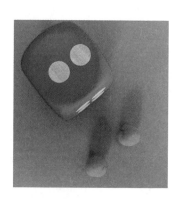

Learning Opportunities

One-to-one correspondence
Number recognition
Small-motor skills

Materials

Playdough mats or construction paper
Clear sheet protectors
Playdough
Dice

What to Do

Download printable playdough mats free from the internet, or create your own from construction paper. Insert the mats into clear sheet protectors. Give the children dice, and encourage each child to roll a die and then use playdough to make a set of that many objects of their choice on the mat.

Shapes Mats

Learning Opportunities

Shape recognition

Small-motor skills

Materials

Playdough mats or paper

Markers

Clear sheet protectors

Playdough

What to Do

Download printable playdough mats free from the internet, or create your own. Draw a circle, square, rectangle, triangle, and other shapes on the mats. Slide the mats into clear sheet protectors. Encourage the children to roll the playdough to match with the shapes on the mats. For an added challenge, invite the children to make solid (3-D) shapes, such as a sphere, cube, rectangular prism, tetrahedron, and so on with playdough.

Measurement Mats

Learning Opportunities

Spatial recognition

Comparing

Small-motor skills

Materials

Playdough mats or construction paper

Clear sheet protectors

Playdough

What to Do

Download printable playdough mats free from the internet, or create your own from construction paper. Insert the mats into clear sheet protectors. Invite the children to make snakes from playdough. Then challenge them to make them longer, then shorter. Engage them in conversations about different measurement words.

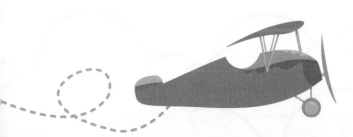

3-D Structures

Learning Opportunities

Engineering skills
Eye-hand coordination
Small-muscle strength
Creativity

Materials

Playdough mats
Toothpicks
Child-safe scissors
Plastic knives
Craft sticks
Straws
Chenille stems
Playdough

What to Do

Put out the materials. Invite the children to plan, construct, and create 3-D structures, over and over again.

Color Mixing

Learning Opportunities

Small-motor skills
Predicting
Testing hypotheses

Materials

Playdough mats
Plain, noncolored playdough
Food coloring

What to Do

Use your favorite recipe to make a batch of playdough. Separate the batch into three parts. Color one part red, one part yellow, and one part blue.

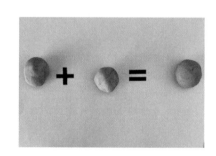

Invite the children to take pinches of the primary colors and squeeze them together in different combinations. Ask them to predict what secondary color they will create with each combination. What colors do they create? Did they predict the correct colors?

Playdough Impressions

Learning Opportunities

Observation skills
Interest in nature
Small-motor skills
Investigation

Materials

Playdough
Natural items

What to Do

Give each child a ball of playdough. Demonstrate how to press the playdough on tree bark, rocks, and other natural objects to make prints. Children can make pancakes with the playdough and then press natural objects on them to make imprints. Encourage children to describe the details they notice. Can they tell what an object is from the print?

Playdough Habitats

Learning Opportunities

Observation skills
Interest in nature
Small-motor skills

Materials

Playdough
Plastic toy animals
Natural items, such as leaves, twigs, rocks, shells, feathers, pinecones, and nuts

What to Do

Invite the children to collect leaves, twigs, rocks, shells, feathers, pinecones, nuts, and other natural objects outside. Encourage them to use their found items and playdough to create different scenes for the plastic animals.

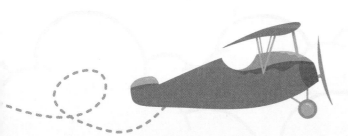

CHAPTER

4

Literacy
Center

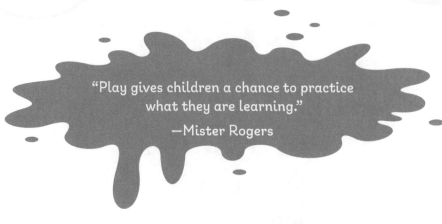

"Play gives children a chance to practice
what they are learning."
—Mister Rogers

A print-rich classroom environment will help children make the connection that print is meaningful and functional. Researchers Michelle Neumann, Michelle Hood, and Ruth Ford (2012) suggest adding labels, charts, signs, packaging, and other print-rich materials to classrooms to provide lots of opportunities for engaging in literacy.

In the literacy center, children can develop reading-readiness skills through hands-on activities and games. Nurture oral

language, phonological awareness, alphabet knowledge, and print knowledge in fun and meaningful ways to help children fall in love with letters, sounds, and learning to read.

The literacy center (or reading center) should be in a quiet area of the classroom and should have a table, chairs, and shelves for storing materials. Consider these items for different skills you are working on.

Materials for the Literacy Center

- Storytelling/oral language:
    - » Puppets
    - » Flannel board
    - » Photo puppets of children
    - » Stuffed animals
    - » Masks
    - » Storybooks
- Alphabet knowledge:
    - » Magnetic letters and cookie sheet
    - » Alphabet blocks
    - » Letter stamps, stamp pad
    - » Letter stickers
    - » Letter tiles
    - » Letter beads
    - » Sponge letters
    - » Phonics games

- Print knowledge:
    - » Fly swatters
    - » Flashlights
    - » Pointers
    - » Silly glasses
    - » Pocket chart
    - » Children's name cards with photos
    - » Small chalkboards or dry-erase boards
    - » Chalk or dry-erase markers
    - » Magic slate
    - » Paper, pencils
    - » Word/picture cards
    - » Picture dictionary
    - » Word puzzles
- Phonological awareness:
    - » Rhyming games
    - » Nursery-rhyme books

Letter Man

Learning Opportunities

Letter recognition
Print knowledge
Writing

Materials

Small swing-lid trashcan
Googly eyes
Pompom
Felt scraps
Scissors
Craft glue

What to Do

Decorate the trashcan with googly eyes and a pompom nose to create Letter Man. Cut out and glue on felt scraps to make his hair, mouth, clothes, and other details. Use Letter Man for some of the activities below.

Letter Assessment

Learning Opportunities

Letter recognition

Materials

Letter Man

Magnetic or foam letters

What to Do

Tell the children that you are going to name some letters. If they know what a letter looks like, they can feed it to Letter Man. As you call out letters, you'll quickly be able to see what letters they know.

Spelling Names

Learning Opportunities

Letter recognition

Emerging spelling

Materials

Letter Man

Magnetic or foam letters

Sentence strips

Marker

What to Do

Ask each child to spell her name using the letters and then feed her name to Letter Man.

If a child needs support, write her name on a sentence strip so she'll have something to copy.

For a greater challenge, ask children to spell their last names or sight words.

Pick a Letter

Learning Opportunities

Letter recognition

Materials

Letter Man
Magnetic or foam letters

What to Do

Place all the letters in Letter Man. Encourage the children to take turns with their friends choosing letters and identifying them. For a challenge, invite the children to make the sounds of the letters as they identify them. Ask them to think of something that begins with each sound.

Pick and Write

Learning Opportunities

Letter recognition
Writing

Materials

Letter Man
Magnetic or foam letters
Paper
Pencil or marker

What to Do

Place the letters in Letter Man. Invite the children to take turns choosing letters and then trying to write the letters.

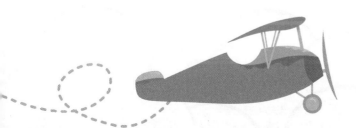

Teddy Bear Letter Match

Learning Opportunities

Color recognition
Matching upper- and lowercase letters
Phonics

Materials

Construction paper in multiple colors
Spring-type clothespins
Scissors
Marker
Shoebox

What to Do

Trace a bear shape and a shirt shape on construction paper. Write uppercase letters on the bears and lowercase letters on the shirts. Cut bears and shirts out of the same colors. Put the bears and shirts in a shoebox with the clothespins.

Invite each child to choose a bear and then use a clothespin to attach the shirt with the lowercase letter that matches the uppercase letter on the bear.

For a challenge, put pictures on the bears and ask the children to choose the shirts that match the beginning sounds of the pictures. Use images such as a ball, a pencil, a dog, a cat, and a sun.

Letter Laundry

Learning Opportunities

Letter recognition
Sight words

Materials

Construction paper
Scissors
Spring-type clothespins
String
Marker

What to Do

Trace outlines of different types of clothing onto different colors of construction paper. Cut out the clothing shapes. Write letters you want the children to practice on the clothes. Tie a string between two chairs for a clothesline. Spread the clothes on the floor or a table. Invite each child to choose a piece of clothing, name the letter, and then hang it on the clothesline.

For a challenge, write sight words on the clothing for children to read and then hang up.

Name Puzzles

Learning Opportunities

Print knowledge
Letter recognition
Name recognition

Materials

Sentence strips
Envelopes
Marker
Scissors
Children's photos
Glue
Dot stickers in two different colors
Unifix cubes
Class directory

What to Do

Write each child's name on a sentence strip. Cut between the letters to make a puzzle. Next, write each child's name and glue the child's photo on an envelope. Place the puzzle pieces inside the envelope. Children can practice putting the puzzles together and reading their names and their friends' names.

For more fun, put dot stickers on Unifix cubes. Use one color for the first letter and same-colored dots for the other letters. For example, use a red dot for the first letter, and green dots for the remaining letters. Print the letters in children's names on the dots. Put a class directory with names and pictures nearby, so children can practice "building" their friends' names.

Pull and Read

Learning Opportunities

Print knowledge
Left-to-right orientation
Name recognition

Materials

Envelopes
Sentence strips
Children's photos
Markers
Glue

What to Do

Write the children's names on 12-inch sentence strips, and glue each child's photo on the right end of his name strip. Cut the left end off of the envelopes and insert one sentence strip inside each envelope.

Invite the children to pull out a strip to expose one letter at a time and to blend the sounds as they pull. Ask them to predict whose name it might be. They can self-check by pulling the strip all the way out and seeing their friend's photo.

For more challenge, write color words with a black marker on sentence strips and make a small dot to match the color on the right end. Children can pull out one letter at a time and try to read the color word. They can self-check with the color dot at the end.

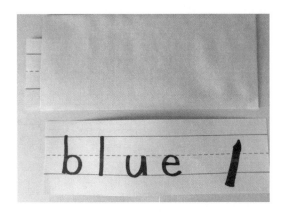

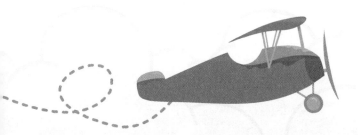

Name Bracelets

Learning Opportunities

Letter recognition
Name recognition
Small-motor skills

Materials

Alphabet beads
Chenille stems
Sentence strips
Marker

What to Do

Put out the alphabet beads and chenille stems.
Encourage the children to find the letters in their
names and thread them on the chenille stems. They
can twist the ends together to make bracelets.

For children who need support, write their names on
sentence strips so they will have an example to go by.
For children who need a challenge, ask them to add the
letters in their last names to their bracelets.

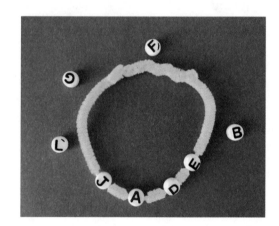

Clothespin Letters and Words

Learning Opportunities

Small-motor skills
Print knowledge
Name recognition
Sight words

Materials

Spring-type clothespins
Jumbo craft sticks
Children's photos
Marker

What to Do

Write each child's name on a jumbo craft stick, and glue the child's photo at the end. Write each letter of the child's name on a different clothespin. Invite the children to attach the clothespins, letter by letter, to their name craft sticks.

For more fun, write color words on craft sticks and have children match up the clothespin letters to make color words.

For children who need a challenge, use this activity to reinforce sight words. Ask children to write the words after matching up the clothespins.

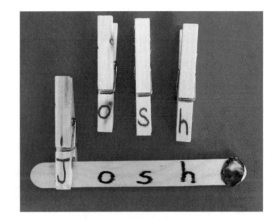

Letter Bags and Boxes

Learning Opportunities

Environmental print
Letter recognition
Visual discrimination

Materials

Branded bags from restaurants
Empty food boxes
Magnetic or foam letters
Scissors
Basket

What to Do

Cut the fronts off the food boxes. Set out the box fronts and food bags. Place the foam letters or magnetic letters in a basket. Invite the children to pick letters and then try to match them with the same letters on a bag or box.

For more challenge, ask the children to find words that they can read on the bags or boxes.

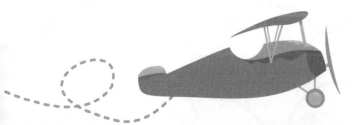

Letter Pops

Learning Opportunities

Letter recognition
Phonics
Environmental print

Materials

Jumbo craft sticks
Magnetic letters
Craft glue (such as E6000) (Adult use only)
Small can or pail

What to Do

In a well-ventilated area away from the children, glue a magnetic letter to each jumbo craft stick to make letter pops. Put the dry letter pops in a can or pail. Invite the children to choose letters and then try to match them up with environmental print in the classroom. For more fun, place the letter pops in your classroom library so the children can match up letters in books.

For a challenge, ask each child to find something in the classroom that begins with the sound of the letter.

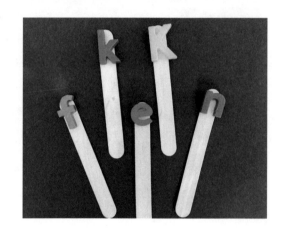

Letter Cups

Learning Opportunities

Matching upper- and lowercase letters
Sight words

Materials

Plastic bathroom cups
Permanent markers or letter stickers

What to Do

Write uppercase letters on some of the cups and matching lowercase letters on other cups. Start with five to ten letters, and increase the number as the children become more proficient. Invite the children to stack the matching uppercase and lowercase letters together. For more fun, tell the children that if they know a letter, they can use that cup to build a pyramid. Hint: an empty potato-chip can is perfect for storing the cups.

For children who need more support, trace around the bottom of a cup on a file folder to make circles. Write an uppercase letter in each circle. Encourage the children to set the cups with the lowercase letters on the matching circles.

For a challenge, invite the children to spell out their names or other words with the cups.

Peeking Puppies

Learning Opportunities

Name recognition
Upper- and lowercase letters
Phonics

Materials

Construction paper
Scissors
Markers
Glue

What to Do

Trace the shape of a puppy with upright ears onto full-sized sheets of construction paper. Make one puppy for each child in your class. Cut out the puppies, then bend down one ear on each. Write a child's name on each puppy's body. Lift the folded ear, and glue on a photo of the child. Invite the children to try to read the name on a puppy. They can check themselves by looking under the ear to see if they said the right name. For more fun, write an uppercase letter on the puppy's body. Have children try to write the corresponding lowercase letter and self-check by looking at the corresponding lowercase letter under the ear.

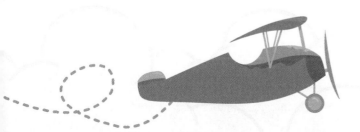

For a challenge, glue a picture to the puppy's body. Use images such as a ball, a pencil, fruit, a dog, a cat, and a sun. Lift the ear and write the letter that matches the beginning sound of the picture.

 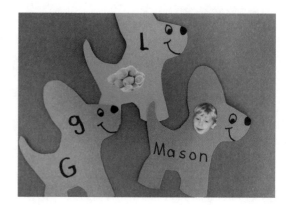

Puzzlers

Learning Opportunities

Rhyming words
Upper- and lowercase letters
Phonics

Materials

Paper plates
Rhyming pictures
Markers
Scissors
Glue
Ziplock bag

What to Do

Cut paper plates in half using puzzle designs similar to those shown. Glue pictures that rhyme on each half, such as *bee* and *tree*, *dog* and *frog*, and *run* and *bun*. Write each word under its corresponding picture. Mix up the pieces. Invite the children to say the words and match up the plate halves that rhyme. Store the puzzlers in a ziplock bag. The game is self-checking because the pieces will fit if the children match the correct pictures.

For more fun, make puzzlers for matching uppercase and lowercase letters.

For a challenge, make puzzlers to let the children match pictures and beginning sounds.

Letter Hunt

Learning Opportunities

Letter recognition
Sight words

Materials

Pointers
Empty eyeglass frames

What to Do

Invite the children to put on the glasses and then walk around the room pointing at letters and naming them. Encourage them to use the pointers to read classroom words.

For a challenge, send the children on a letter hunt for each letter in the alphabet.

Hint: You can purchase a pointer, or just make your own by removing the cardboard roll from a pants hanger, rolling it in glue, and dipping it in glitter.

Letters in the Snow

Learning Opportunities

Letter recognition

Writing

Materials

Smooth pebbles
Permanent marker
Tub
Shredded white paper or white sand

What to Do

Write an alphabet letter on each pebble with a permanent marker. Put the pebbles in the tub and add shredded paper or sand to make "snow." Invite the children to find the letters in the snow and to name each letter when they find it. For a challenge, ask the children to write down the letters that they find.

Hint: Put the pebbles in the freezer so they will be cold like snow.

Fronts and Backs

Learning Opportunities

Visual matching
Visual memory

Materials

Empty cereal and food boxes
Scissors

What to Do

Ask families to send in empty food boxes from home. Cut the fronts and backs off the boxes, and trim them to be the same size. Mix them up and ask the children to match the ones that go together. Hint: Start with five pairs and increase the number as the children become more proficient.

For more fun, use the boxes to play a memory game. Place the fronts and backs of the boxes facedown on the floor. Encourage the children to turn over two at a time and try to find a match. Start with five pairs and increase the difficulty as the children become more proficient.

Pony Roundup

Learning Opportunities

Upper- and lowercase letters
Small-motor skills
Rhymes
Phonics

Materials

Construction paper
Markers
Spring-type clothespins

What to Do

Trace ponies (without the legs) and saddles onto construction paper. Cut out the ponies and saddles. Print an uppercase letter on each pony and a lowercase letter on each saddle. Invite the children to clip clothespins onto the pony bodies to make legs, and then to stand them up. Next, invite the children to match the correct saddle to each pony.

Hint: Start with five ponies and saddles and increase the number to make it more challenging. For more fun, put pictures on the ponies and have the children match saddles with the beginning sounds of the pictures. Use images such as a ball, a pencil, a dog, a cat, and a sun.

For even more fun, glue rhyming pictures such as *bee* and *tree*, *dog* and *log*, *mop* and *stop*, and so on, to the saddles and ponies. Invite the children to match the rhyming words.

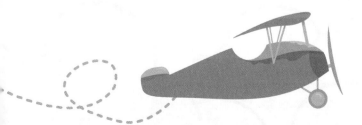

Eggs-Tra

Learning Opportunities

Upper- and lowercase letters
Writing
Phonics

Materials

Plastic eggs
Permanent marker
Basket
Paper
Pencils

What to Do

With a permanent marker, write an uppercase letter on one half of an egg and a lowercase letter on the other half. Take the eggs apart and mix them up in the basket. Invite the children to find matching letters and put them together. For more fun, give them paper and pencils, and ask them to write both the upper- and lowercase letters.

For even more fun, cut out small pictures and glue them onto small pieces of card stock for a beginning sound game. (Laminate or cover with clear contact paper for durability.) Encourage the children to put the appropriate pictures in the eggs with the letters for the beginning sounds.

Memory Rhymes

Learning Opportunities

Rhyming
Visual memory
Visual discrimination
Phonics

Materials

Poster board
Glue
Scissors
Pictures of rhyming words

The Possibilities of Play

What to Do

Cut the poster board into 3 $\frac{1}{2}$" x 4" rectangles. Glue pictures of rhyming words on the rectangles. Invite the children to match up the pictures that rhyme. Then, mix up the cards, turn them facedown, and spread them out in a grid on a table. Invite the children to take turns turning over first one card and then another to see if they rhyme. If the pictures rhyme, the child may keep the match and have another turn. If the pictures don't rhyme, the child should turn them back over and the next child gets a turn.

For children who need support, play this game using matching stickers or pictures (not rhyming ones).

For a challenge, make a matching game where children match uppercase and lowercase letters.

Finger Talk

Learning Opportunities

Alphabet recognition
Small-motor skills

Materials

Images of American Sign Language (ASL) letters
Construction paper
Scissors
Glue
Envelope
File folder
Markers

What to Do

Cut out the images of the ASL letters and glue them onto 2 $\frac{1}{2}$" x 2 $\frac{1}{2}$" construction-paper squares. Write the upper- and lowercase letters for each on the bottom right corner of the squares. Put them in an envelope. Write the upper- and lowercase letters on construction-paper squares. Invite the children to match the ASL signs with the corresponding letters.

For more fun, print another set of ASL letters and label the letters with a marker. Glue these on the inside of a file folder. Encourage the children to match the signs with the signs on the folder. Invite them to make the ASL letters with their fingers.

For children who need support, limit the number of letters the children need to match.

For a challenge, encourage the children to make ASL signs when you sing alphabet songs. Invite them to spell their names or sight words with sign language.

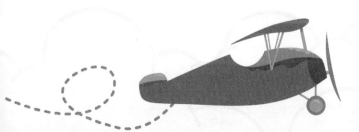

Configuration Station

Learning Opportunities

Visual discrimination
Color words

Materials

File folder
Color words
Paper
Marker

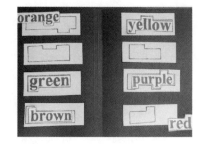

What to Do

Print out color words in a large font. Cut out the words. On paper, trace around the shape of each word to create an outline. Cut out the outlines, and glue the word outline shapes onto a file folder. Invite the children to match the color words with their word outline shapes. Challenge them to read some of the words.

For children who need more support, trace over the color words with a marker in the appropriate color.

For a challenge, make word-shapes puzzles of children's names or sight words.

Environmental Print

Learning Opportunities

Print knowledge
Visual memory
Tracking print

Materials

Food labels, logos from toys, advertisements, and so on
Scissors
Index cards
Marker
Glue

The Possibilities of Play

What to Do

Cut out the logos and labels and glue them on index cards. For each child, write *I* on one index card and *like* on another index card. Invite the children to lay the *I like* index cards on a table and then choose a picture with the environmental print of something that they like. After placing the picture at the end of the index cards, encourage them to point and read, "I like [word or logo]."

For a challenge, invite the children to take turns doing this with a friend.

For more fun, tape examples of environmental print to the classroom door. Every time children go in and out, encourage them to point to a word or logo that they can read.

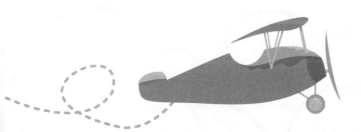

Writing Center

> "The playing adult steps sideward into another reality; the playing child advances forward to new stages of mastery."
>
> —Erik H. Erikson, developmental psychologist, *Childhood and Society*

Emergent literacy will flourish in a writing center. Children will develop a positive attitude about writing by using a variety of blank books and tools. Remember, scribbles are how the writing process begins, so whatever the children do should be celebrated.

Research has shown that children will naturally engage in emergent writing activities as part of their play. For example, Deborah Rowe and Carin Neitzel (2010) found that young children will explore writing materials based on their interests. If a child is interested in a particular topic, he will use writing materials to explore and "record" his ideas. If a child is interested in how writing works, he will explore using different writing materials and will try to write alphabet letters. Children with creative interests will explore different writing materials and their uses in a variety of ways. Children who are socially oriented will use emergent writing to connect with peers through play together. These findings open up opportunities for the teacher to engage different

children in exploring writing by observing how individuals connect with writing and then capitalizing on that interest with center opportunities. Keep your writing center well stocked with lots of different materials. Also, add writing materials to other centers, such as dramatic play or science, to give children opportunities to incorporate emergent writing into their play and explorations.

Materials for the Writing Center

Table and chairs	Dry-erase board, markers, and erasers
Pens, pencils, crayons, markers	Magic slate
Variety of paper: colored, notepads, different shapes and sizes	Stamps and ink pad
Envelopes	Child-safe scissors, tape, stapler
Blank books	Picture file
Sticky notes	Picture dictionary
Junk mail	Class list
Book order forms, magazine inserts, tax forms (available at a public library)	Magnetic letters
Small chalkboards and chalk	Clipboard
	Used greeting cards
	Old mailbox

Class Directory

Learning Opportunities

Small-motor skills
Prewriting
Letter recognition

Materials

Index cards
Marker
Children's photos
Small box
Hole punch
Metal ring

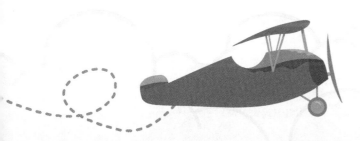

What to Do

Print each child's name on an index card, and glue the child's photo next to his name. Store the cards in a small box, or punch holes in the cards and hang them on a book ring. Place the directory in the writing center, and encourage each child to copy a friend's name on a piece of paper and write a letter to that friend. Let students put their letters in the center's mailbox.

Seasonal Picture Dictionary

Learning Opportunities

Small-motor skills
Prewriting
Letter recognition
Vocabulary

Materials

Paper
Construction paper
Glue
Hole punch
Book rings
Markers
Pictures to reflect a season, holiday, or theme

What to Do

On a piece of paper, write a few words that relate to the season or a holiday or another topic that your students are learning about. Next to each word, draw or glue a picture to represent the word. Cut a decorative edge on the paper if you like, and glue it onto a piece of construction paper. Punch holes down the left side of the pages, and bind them together with book rings. Post the dictionary in the writing center, and read the words with the children. Encourage them to use the words in letters, stories, or other writing they create in the center.

Pencil Grip

Learning Opportunities

Small-motor skills
Prewriting

Materials

Silly bands or ponytail bands
Pencils
Paper

What to Do

Tell the children that you are going to create a seatbelt for a pencil. Show the children how to put a silly band (or ponytail band) around the wrist of the hand they write with. Explain, "When you go somewhere in the car, you put on a seatbelt. When you write, you need to put a seatbelt on your pencil." Hold the pencil and loop the rest of silly band around it so that their pointer and middle fingers are holding the pencil and their ring and pinky fingers are curled into their palms. "Now, Mom and Dad are in the front seat, and the kids are in the back seat." It's amazing how much more control children will have with their writing instrument using this technique.

> It will help children to learn to write if they understand how to hold their pencils correctly. You don't want to force a child, but do model these techniques and encourage children to try them when they write.

Pompom Finger Pillow

Learning Opportunities

Small-motor skills
Prewriting

Materials

Small pompoms or cotton balls
Pencils
Paper

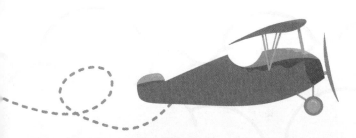

What to Do

Give each child a pompom or cotton ball to hold in his hand when he writes. Demonstrate how to put his pinky and ring finger to "sleep" on the pompom before picking up the pencil.

Writing Bracelet

Learning Opportunities

Small-motor skills
Prewriting

Materials

Beads
Jingle bells
Yarn or string
Scissors

What to Do

Cut pieces of yarn or string long enough so that, when each is tied in a loop, it will slide easily off a child's wrist and hand. String a bead or jingle bell on each piece of yarn or string, and tie the ends of the string to make a bracelet.

Show the children how to hold the bead or jingle bell in their hand as they write. The object helps the child hold her pencil correctly.

The Possibilities of Play

Emergent Writing

As children are exposed to print in the environment, they begin to understand that writing is a way of communicating. Children explore communicating in this way through drawing and scribbling, making letter-like forms, and writing random strings of letters. (Mayer, 2007).

These skills can be nurtured through some of the multisensory activities you create in your writing center. Teachers can also support children's skill development by modeling writing and by scaffolding children's attempts at writing (Gerde, Bingham, and Wasik, 2012; Quinn, Gerde, and Bingham, 2016).

> **Tip:** Have the children wash their hands before and after using sensory materials.

Sensory Tub

Learning Opportunities

Small-motor skills
Eye-hand coordination
Emergent writing skills

Materials

Plastic tub with lid
Sand, water beads, aquarium rocks, salt, or other sensory materials
Card stock
Markers
Paper
Clear contact paper

What to Do

Fill the bottom of a plastic tub with sand, water beads, aquarium rocks, salt, or another sensory material. Invite the children to practice making shapes and letters in the tub.

For more fun, make copycat cards of examples of words or letters. Place these copycat cards near the sensory tub or the sandbox on the playground. Children can look at these cards and try to copy each word or letter in the sensory tub or sandbox.

For a challenge, make mystery shapes. Draw a large shape or letter with a dark marker on a sheet of paper. Cover the paper with clear contact paper. Place the mystery shape in the bottom of the tub and cover it with the sensory material. Children can sift through the tub to find the mystery shape, then they can trace over that shape.

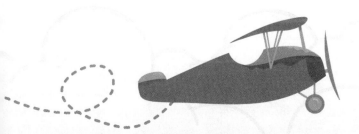

Rainbow Writing

Learning Opportunities

Small-motor skills
Prewriting
Repetition

Materials

Paper
Markers, crayons
Chart paper
Tape
Sidewalk chalk

What to Do

Use a black marker to make letters, numbers, shapes, and names on the paper. Invite the children to use different markers or crayons to trace these in multiple colors. For more fun, do rainbow writing, using several markers or crayons at once, with letters, numbers, shapes, and names. For even more fun, make giant letters and shapes on chart paper, and tape them to a wall. Encourage the children to work together to make rainbows on the shapes using rainbow writing.

Outside, draw shapes on a paved surface with sidewalk chalk. Encourage the children to trace the shapes with chalk.

Shaving Cream

Learning Opportunities

Small-motor development
Prewriting

Materials

Non-menthol shaving cream
Lunchroom trays or a laminated tabletop

What to Do

Squirt the shaving cream on the tray or tabletop. Let the children explore the texture of the shaving cream. After free exploration, encourage them to practice making shapes and letters.

For outside fun, spray shaving cream on plastic trays on a picnic table. Invite the children to explore the shaving cream.

Left to Right

Left-to-right orientation is a key to beginning reading and writing. Here are some activities children can do to develop directionality.

Writing Trails

Learning Opportunities

Small-motor skills
Left-to-right orientation
Task initiation and completion

Materials

Sentence strips
Toy cars
Small plastic animals
Markers
Large sheets of paper
Sidewalk chalk

What to Do

Draw tracks on sentence strips similar to the ones shown in the photo. Children can drive cars or move animals by following the tracks from left to right. To help them understand where to start and where to finish, make a green dot where they are to begin and a red dot where they should end.

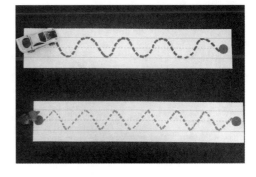

For more fun, give the children large sheets of paper, add the green and red dots, and let them draw their own trails from left to right.

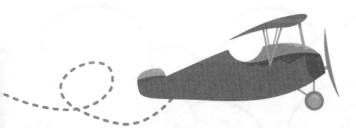

Outside, draw tracks in sand or with chalk on the sidewalk. Invite children to move toy vehicles over the tracks from left to right.

Walking Pencils

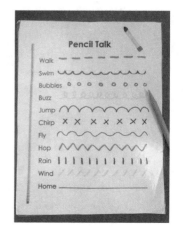

Learning Opportunities

Left-to-right orientation
Small-motor skills

Materials

Paper
Green crayon, red crayon
Pencils

What to Do

Draw a vertical green line down the left side of a sheet of paper. Draw a red line down the right side. Give the children pencils and have them practice "walking their pencils" (making a long line without picking up the pencil) from the green line to the red line. Remind them when they get to the red line they should stop, pick up their pencils, and go back to the green line.

For more fun, demonstrate how the pencils can skip (make short, horizontal lines), hop (make curves up and down), gallop (make a short slanted line, like a slash mark), and stomp (make a short vertical line). Can they make their pencils mark in all those different ways from one side to the other?

Ready to Write

Children grow and develop at different rates and ways over time. This is particularly true when it comes to asking prekindergarten children to write. They need many multisensory opportunities to play and work with forming letters and numbers before correct formation becomes natural for them.

Highway Shapes and Letters

Learning Opportunities

Letter recognition
Small-motor skills
Prewriting

Materials

Highway shapes
Letters
Numerals
Clear sheet protectors
Toy cars
Dry-erase markers
Playdough
Masking tape
Sidewalk chalk

What to Do

Download and print highway shapes, letters, and numerals (free at www.makinglearningfun.com), or make your own. Laminate the highway shapes or place them in clear sheet protectors. Give the children toy cars, and invite them to drive on the highways. Use a green dot to indicate where children should begin. Put a red dot or checkered flag where they should end.

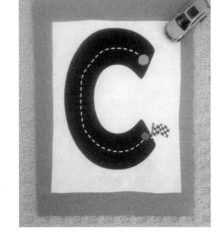

Laminate or place the letters and numerals in sheet protectors. Give the children toy cars and invite them to drive on the letters and numerals. Use a green dot to indicate where they should begin. Put a red dot where they should end.

For more fun, let the children trace lines on the highways with dry-erase markers and then erase them. Or, let the children roll playdough into "snakes" and put these on top of the highways.

For even more fun, make letters, shapes, and numbers with masking tape on the floor for children to drive over with toy cars.

Outside, use sidewalk chalk to make letters and shapes on a paved surface for children to drive over with toy vehicles.

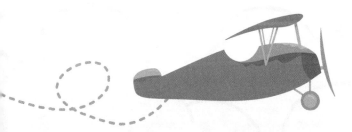

Playdough Plates

Learning Opportunities

Letter recognition
Small-motor skills

Materials

Clear plastic plates
Permanent marker
Playdough

What to Do

Draw shapes and letters on clear plastic plates with a permanent marker. Invite the children to roll or cut playdough and place it on top of the lines.

For a challenge, ask children to make an object that begins with the sound of a letter on the plate.

Lotty Dotty

Learning Opportunities

Sensorimotor skills
Alphabet recognition
Writing

Materials

School glue
Heavy paper
Water-based marker

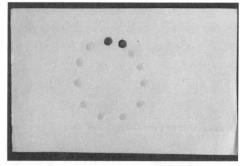

What to Do

Use a marker to make shapes and letters with dots instead of lines; make the first dot green and the last dot red to indicate where to start and stop. Put a drop of glue on top of each dot and let dry.

Invite the children to trace over the dots of glue with their fingers. Encourage them to whisper the letter or shape names as they trace them. For a challenge, ask children to write the letters after tracing over them.

For more fun, place a sheet of paper on top of the dots. Remove the paper wrap from a crayon, and rub over the dots with the side of the crayon. Ask the children to use crayons to connect the dots to make the letters.

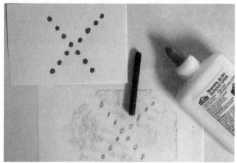

Textured Writing

Learning Opportunities

Sensory exploration
Small-motor skills
Letter and shape recognition

Materials

Plastic needlepoint canvas or sandpaper
Paper
Crayons

What to Do

You can use sandpaper or plastic needlepoint canvas (available at most craft stores) for textured writing. Place the paper on top of the canvas or sandpaper. Invite the children to use crayons to make shapes or write letters. Tell them to press firmly for the best results. Invite them to trace over the textured crayon marks with their fingers and name the shapes or say the letters.

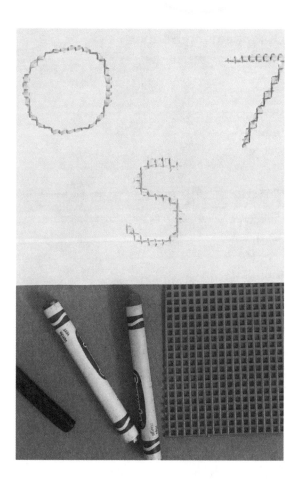

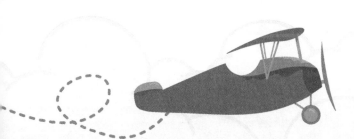

Disappearing Shapes

Learning Opportunities

Small-motor skills
Letter recognition
Writing

Materials

Dark construction paper or small chalkboards
Small cups
Sponges
Scissors
Water
Spring-type clothespins
Flashlights
Sidewalk chalk
Bucket
Paintbrushes

What to Do

Cut the sponges into strips. Give each child a small cup of water and a strip of sponge. If children are reluctant to touch the damp sponges, you can put pieces of sponge in spring-type clothespins, and they can use them like paintbrushes. Have them dip the sponges in the water and practice writing shapes and letters on the dark paper or the chalkboards. As the water evaporates, the shapes and letters will "disappear."

For more fun, give children flashlights and have them lie on their backs and practice making shapes and letters on the ceiling.

Outside, let children paint shapes and letters on the sidewalk with paintbrushes and bucket of water. Or, let them use sidewalk chalk to practice writing on a paved surface.

Clipboard Cruising

Learning Opportunities

Motivation to write

Writing skills

Materials

Corrugated cardboard

Scissors

Bulldog clips

Paper

Pencils

What to Do

Cut the cardboard into 9" x 12" pieces. Let children make their own clipboards by decorating the cardboard with their names and drawings. Attach a bulldog clip at the top of each clipboard, and insert paper. Children can walk around the room and copy the shapes, letters, numbers, and so on, that they see.

For a challenge, let them use clipboards to take surveys. Draw a line down the middle of a sheet of paper. Write *cats* on one side and *dogs* on the other. Children can interview their classmates to see whether they like cats or dogs better. Teach them how to make tally marks to record friends' favorites.

For more fun, they can do similar surveys of favorite flavors of ice cream, pizza toppings, books, songs, and so on.

Outside, give children clipboards on the playground, and encourage them to draw clouds, trees, and other natural items.

I'm a Writer. I'm an Author.

How exciting to give a young child a blank book and invite her to be a writer! Just as a baby babbles before words come out, children must scribble before they can write letters and words (Byington and Kim, 2017). Blank books are open ended, so children can be successful at any level. The following are ideas for simple books you can prepare ahead of time to entice children to be authors. As they scribble and use creative spelling, children will nurture writing skills and be motivated to read. These books can be used for open-ended writing, but they can also be used to reinforce alphabet knowledge, science, and math standards.

Also, consider that many children don't have books in their homes, so making books at school and sending them home is a special way to connect with families. Try letting children dictate stories as you write them down word for word. They can then decorate their storybooks and share them with their families. Children will love seeing their stories in print.

Book Boxes

Learning Opportunities

Motivation to write and read
Writing skills
Letter recognition
Small-motor skills
Book-handling skills
Home-school connection
Self-confidence
Creativity

Materials

Empty cereal boxes
Stickers
Tempera paint
Paintbrushes
Markers
Other art
media

What to Do

Ask families to send in empty cereal boxes from home.

Invite the children to paint the boxes or decorate them with stickers and other art media. They can use these boxes as personal libraries to save the books that they make.

Place completed books, blank books, and pencils in the book boxes, so the children can read the books they've made or write new ones.

For more fun, spray paint* the boxes gold or silver to make treasure boxes for books.

*Safety note: Use the spray paint in a well-ventilated area away from the children.

Basic Blank Book

Learning Opportunities

Motivation to write and read
Writing skills
Letter recognition
Small-motor skills
Book-handling skills

Materials

Construction paper
Paper
Stapler
Pencils, crayons, and other writing tools
Glue sticks

What to Do

Fold two sheets of paper in half and staple along the fold. If you wish, use a colored sheet of paper on the outside and fold a white sheet of paper on the inside, then staple along the fold.

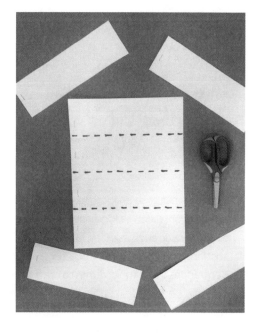

Make enough blank books for each child to have at least one. Place the blank books in the writing center, along with pencils, crayons, and other writing tools. Invite the children to use them for a variety of activities.

- **Phonics**—When studying a letter, instead of giving children a worksheet, have each child make a book about that letter. Children can draw pictures of things that begin with that sound, cut out pictures and glue them in the books, write the letter, write words that contain that letter, and so on.
- **Environmental print**—Have children cut out words they recognize from newspapers and advertisements and glue them in their books.
- **Comprehension**—Ask children to retell a nursery rhyme or story in their books. They can use a combination of drawing, scribbling, and invented spelling.
- **Math**—Invite the children to walk around the room and draw shapes to create shape books. These blank books can also be used for writing numbers and making sets.
- **Names**—Use these books like autograph books, so children can practice writing their names.

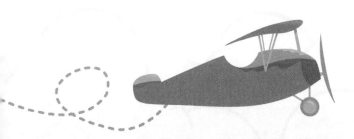

- **Themes**—Coordinate books with a unit or theme. For example, if you are studying birds, children could make bird books. If they are investigating water, they can make books that show ice, water, and steam, as well as ways people use water and fun things they like to do with water. For Thanksgiving, invite them to make books of things they are thankful for.

Brochures

Learning Opportunities

Motivation to write and read
Writing skills
Letter recognition
Small-motor skills

Materials

Paper
Old magazines
Glue
Child-safe scissors
Pencils, crayons, markers, and so on

What to Do

Fold a sheet of paper into thirds and flatten to create a brochure. You can also teach children how to make their own brochures by demonstrating how to roll the paper into a "burrito" and then smash it flat.

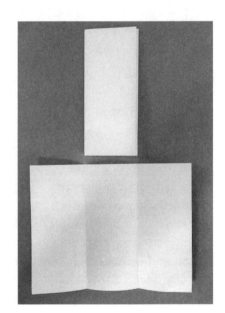

- **Sorting**—Invite the children to cut out magazine pictures in a category (such as foods or animals), sort them by a characteristic such as color, and glue them into different sections.
- **Sequence**—Invite the children to draw what happens at the beginning, middle, and end of a nursery rhyme or story.
- **Names**—Open the brochure so it is portrait style (vertical). Write each child's name on the middle section and ask him to trace over it. The child can fold down the top section and trace over his name again, then fold up the bottom section and trace his name a third time.
- **Field Trip**—If you take a field trip, invite the children to make brochures about it.
- **Units or Themes**—Have children create brochures to show what they learned in a unit of study.

The Possibilities of Play

Itty Bitty Books

Learning Opportunities

Motivation to write and read
Writing skills
Letter recognition
Small-motor skills
Book-handling skills

Materials

Paper
Stapler
Scissors
Pencils, markers, and so on

What to Do

Stack four to six sheets of paper, and staple all four corners.

Cut down the middle lengthwise and widthwise to make four little booklets.

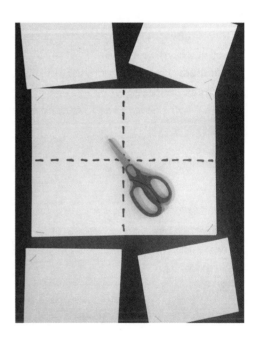

These little books are perfect to place in the writing center for open-ended activities. They can also be used as letter books, number books, shape books, or to reinforce any skill you want children to practice.

For more fun, stack the number of sheets you want, turn the paper horizontally, and staple four times vertically down one short side. Cut across the paper horizontally to make four long, skinny books. Use these for tracing left to right, practicing making letters and shapes, writing names, and so on.

Flip Book

Learning Opportunities

Motivation to write and read
Writing skills
Letter recognition
Small-motor skills

Materials

Paper
Scissors
Pencils, crayons, and so on

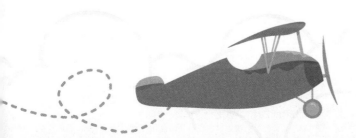

What to Do

Fold the paper in half. (Some call this making a hot dog fold.)

Fold the paper in half again. (Some call this a hamburger fold.)

Fold the paper in half again. (Some call this making a juice box.)

Open the paper, and cut down each crease to the middle fold.

Fold the paper in half again to make four flaps.

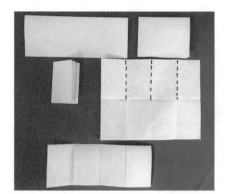

- **Letters**—Invite the children to write alphabet letters on the fronts and draw pictures of objects that begin with that sound on the insides.
- **Rhyming words**—Invite each child to draw pictures of objects that rhyme—one on the front and a rhyming object inside.
- **Numbers**—Invite the children to write numbers on the fronts and then draw that many objects inside.
- **Animals**—Invite each child to draw a mother animal on the fronts and baby animals on the insides, or an animal on the front of a flap and its home on the inside.

House Book

Learning Opportunities

Motivation to write and read
Writing skills
Letter recognition
Small-motor skills

Materials

Paper
Crayons, markers, and so on

What to Do

Fold a piece of paper in half lengthwise, and make a crease.

Open the paper. Bring the upper-left corner to the center, and crease.

Bring the upper-right corner to the center, and crease.

Fold up the bottom edge to make a house shape.

- **My family**—Children can draw pictures of their families, how they celebrate special occasions, how they have fun together, and so on.

- **Shapes**—Each child can draw a shape on the front and then draw objects of that shape on the inside of the book.
- **Phonics**—Invite each child to write an uppercase and lowercase letter on the front of the house and then open and draw pictures that begin with that sound on the inside.
- **Recall**—After reading a story, invite the children to draw their favorite parts on the insides of their houses.

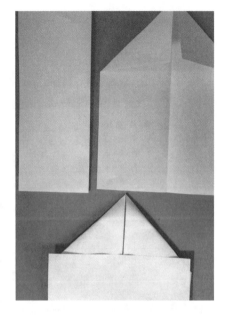

Napkin Book

Learning Opportunities

Motivation to write and read
Writing skills
Letter recognition
Small-motor skills
Book-handling skills

Materials

Holiday or seasonal paper napkins
Paper
Stapler
Scissors
Pencils, crayons, markers, and so on

What to Do

Purchase holiday or seasonal paper napkins at a dollar store. Cut pieces of paper to the size of a napkin for each child. Insert the pieces of paper between the folds of the napkin; the napkin will make a book cover and the paper will make the pages. Staple along the napkin fold to make a book.

Invite the children to write or draw anything they wish that reminds them of the holiday or season.

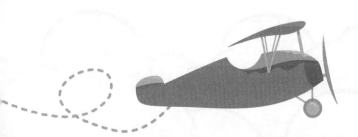

Math
Center

> "Children learn as they play. Most importantly in play children learn how to learn."
> —O. Fred Donaldson, play researcher and author

Research tells us that math is important in early childhood. Early math predicts later school success (Clements and Sarama, 2014). In your math center, children will have opportunities to count, sort, make patterns, measure, explore shapes, make comparisons, and join and separate sets in the math center. They will also develop their small-motor, problem-solving, and social skills.

Create a special area in your classroom where children can discover and reinforce their understanding of math concepts. Include a table, a shelf, and containers to store materials in this area. Label each container with the name and a picture of the item. Relate counters and math manipulatives to seasons or themes. For example, if you are doing an ocean unit, offer the children shells to count and sort. In the fall, you might want to include leaves in the math center.

Model how to use the materials and how to clean up. Begin by putting out one material at a time. When children have learned how to use one material and then clean up, add another. Children should have several choices, but don't overwhelm them with too many materials at once.

Materials for the Math Center

- Counters
  - » Shells
  - » Rocks
  - » Buttons
  - » Toothpicks
  - » Keys
  - » Bottle caps
  - » Paint chips
  - » Erasers
  - » Small toys
  - » Craft sticks
  - » Birthday candles
  - » Hairbows
  - » Small cars
  - » Crayons
  - » Party favors
  - » Leaves
- Sorting
  - » Sorting box
  - » Divided serving dishes
  - » Flannel board and felt pieces
- One-to-one correspondence
  - » Muffin pan
  - » Ice-cube tray

- Numbers
  - » Dice
  - » Deck of cards
  - » Number puzzles
  - » Tactile numerals
  - » Dominoes
  - » Board games
  - » Dot cards
  - » 10 frame
  - » Number poster
  - » Play phone
- Patterns
  - » Pattern blocks
  - » Sewing beads
  - » Pegboard and pegs
  - » Unifix cubes
- Writing
  - » Small chalkboards
  - » Dry-erase board
  - » Dry-erase markers
  - » Paper
  - » Pencils
- Counting
  - » Dice
  - » Number line
  - » Hundreds chart
  - » Counting cubes

- » Abacus
- » Counting books
- Geometry
  - » Geoboard
  - » Felt shapes
  - » Attribute blocks
  - » 3-D shapes
- Time
  - » Toy clock
  - » Stopwatch
  - » Minute timer
- Money
  - » Play money
  - » US coins
  - » Foreign coins
  - » Coupons
- Measurement
  - » Ruler
  - » Tape measure
  - » Balance scale
  - » Measuring cups and spoons
- Addition
  - » Unifix cubes
  - » Calculator
  - » Games

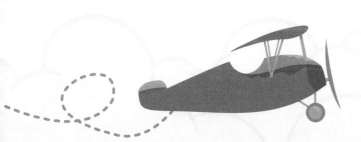

Math Mats

Learning Opportunities

Counting
Making patterns
One-to-one correspondence
Operations
Small-motor skills

Materials

Card stock
Clear sheet protectors
Small and large ziplock bags
Images and counters for different themes, for example:

- Birthday cake: Real candles
- Dog: Small dog bones
- Spaghetti: Pompoms for meatballs
- Face with hair: Barrettes
- Zoo: Small plastic animals

- Jar: Small plastic bugs
- House or car: Keys
- Milkshake: Paper straws
- Bathtub: Glass gems as bubbles
- Piggy bank: Pennies
- Mailbox: Envelopes or junk-mail letters

What to Do

Search the internet for large images, and print them on card stock. Laminate or place the images in clear sheet protectors to make math mats. (You can also trace and cut out your own images for math mats.) Store the mats in large ziplock bags and the counters in a smaller ziplock bags. Invite the children to use the mats and counters for a variety of activities.

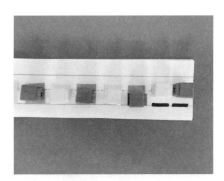

- Have children practice making sets.
  - » Write the numbers 1 to 10 on index cards. Ask the children to choose number cards and then place that number of counters on the math mats.
  - » Give children dot cards, and ask them to reproduce the same number with items on the math mats.
- Patterns—Make pattern cards for children to extend with counters.
- Addition and subtraction—Give children flash cards and ask them to demonstrate joining and separating sets on the mats.

For outside fun, invite the children to help you collect natural items, such as nuts, leaves, pinecones, or small rocks to use with math mats. You can also relate the mats and counters to seasons and holidays, such as a squirrel with acorns in the fall or a tree with plastic flowers in the spring.

One-to-One Book

Learning Opportunities

One-to-one correspondence
Counting
Small-motor skills

Materials

10 sheets of card stock
Black construction paper
Glue
Book ring
Small items (counting bears, pennies, buttons, and so on)

What to Do

Number each of the card stock pages with a numeral from 1 to 10. Write the numeral at the top of the page and the number word at the bottom. Cut the black construction paper into fifty-five 1-inch squares. Glue the appropriate number of squares on each page. Hole punch the top left-hand corners of the pages and add a book ring to make a book. Ask the children to match the small items one to one with the squares on each page.

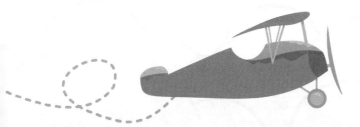

For even more fun, vary this activity by using a variety of objects, such as lacing beads, Unifix cubes, and other small toys.

For a challenge, invite the children to make different combinations for the numbers. For example, on the card stock with the numeral 6, children can place three red bears and three blue buttons or two red bears and four blue buttons on the squares.

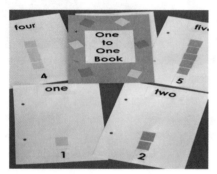
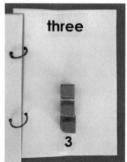

Pattern Book

Learning Opportunities

Extending a pattern
Small-motor skills

Materials

Sentence strips
Markers
Hole punch
Book ring
Counting bears or other manipulatives

What to Do

Draw patterns on the sentence strips with the markers. Start with a simple A-B-A-B pattern and then add A-B-B, A-A-B, and A-B-C patterns. Hole punch the sentence strips and bind them together with the book ring. Ask the children to match the bears with the colors on top of the patterns, and then extend the patterns with the bears.

For a greater challenge, invite each child to play a pattern game with a friend. Ask the first child to make a pattern and encourage the second child to extend it. Then, ask the second child to create a pattern for the first child to extend.

Doing Dots

Learning Opportunities

Subitizing

Small-motor skills

Materials

Dot cards
Pompoms, pebbles, buttons, or other small objects

What to Do

Download and print dot cards from the internet or make your own. Ask the children to match up pompoms, pebbles, buttons, or other small objects with the dots on the cards. Start with cards with one to five dots and, as the children become more proficient, increase the challenge to cards with one to ten dots.

For even more fun, ask the children to attach the appropriate number of paper clips or spring-type clothespins to the dot cards.

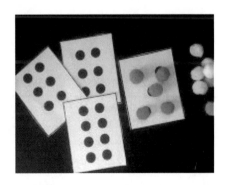

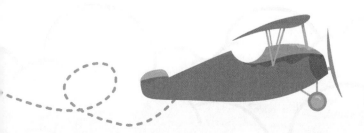

For a greater challenge, make this a game for two children to play. Place dot cards facedown on the table. Ask a child to turn over one card. The first child to say the correct number of dots gets to keep the card. The partner must count the dots to verify that the number is correct.

Number Cups

Learning Opportunities

Counting
Number recognition
Visual matching

Materials

Bathroom cups
Clean, empty potato-chip canister with lid
Permanent marker
File folder

What to Do

Trace around the bottom of a cup on the file folder to make ten circles. Number each of the circles on the folder with a numeral from 1 to 10. Turn the cups upside down and number the bottom of each cup with a numeral from 1 to 10. Mix up the cups and then ask the children to match the numbers on the cups with the numbers on the circles on the file folder. When they've finished playing, ask the children to stack the cups in order and store them in the potato-chip canister.

For children who need more support, start with five cups and then add more as the children become more proficient.

For a greater challenge, encourage the children to practice skip counting, such as counting by tens. Write 10, 20, 30, 40, 50, 60, 70, 80, 90, and 100 in the circles on the file folder and the same

numbers on the cups. Mix up the cups and then ask the children to match the numbers on the cups with the numbers on the circles.

For more fun, write math facts on the sides of the cups. Write the answers to the math facts on the insides of the cups. Ask the children to check their answers by looking inside the cups.

Toy Cars

Learning Opportunities

Cardinality
Matching sets and numbers

Materials

Toy cars
Sticky dots
Permanent marker

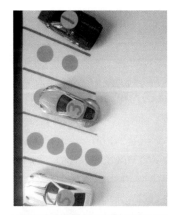

What to Do

Write the numerals 1 to 5 on the sticky dots and then attach them to the cars. Invite the children to "drive" the cars and put them in order. Once the children are successful at putting the cars in order, add more numerals to sticky dots and attach them to more cars.

For even more fun, draw a parking lot on poster board or card stock. Draw different numbers of dots in each space. Encourage the children to "park" their numbered cars with the matching parking spaces.

For a greater challenge, draw a road on a piece of poster board. Mark spaces along the road. Ask the children to roll one die and then move their car that number of spaces.

For outside fun, invite the children to line up the cars on the playground. They can also race their cars by placing two cars at the top of the slide to see which one will come down first.

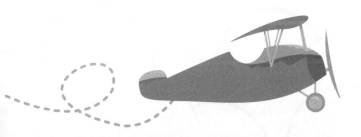

Dealer's Choice

Learning Opportunities

Sorting
Visual discrimination
Cardinality
Inequalities

Materials

Deck of playing cards

What to Do

To develop children's sorting skills, ask the children to sort the cards by suit. Invite them to sort the cards in another way, such as by number or by color.

To help the children understand cardinality, first remove the face cards from the deck. Ask the children to put the remaining cards in numerical order from 1 to 10. (Be sure to explain that an ace is a one, because it has one picture on it.)

For a challenge, draw three columns on a piece of paper and label the columns *high*, *low*, and *equal*. Ask the children to turn over two cards at a time and place the highest number in the *high* pile and the lowest number in the *low* pile. If the cards are equal, the children can place both cards in the *equal* pile. For an even greater challenge, invite the children to select two cards and add up the amount.

Pencil Pocket Book

Learning Opportunities

Sorting
Making sets
Estimating

Materials

5 pencil pockets
Book rings
Small, flat objects (colored craft or ice-pop sticks, poker chips, buttons, flat erasers, and so on)
Sticky notes
Markers

What to Do

Attach the pencil pockets together with book rings to make a book. Write numerals on the sticky notes and attach to the pencil-pocket pages. Ask the children to unzip the pockets, insert the correct number of items, and then zip them shut.

For children who need extra support, start with the numerals 1–5 and increase as children become proficient.

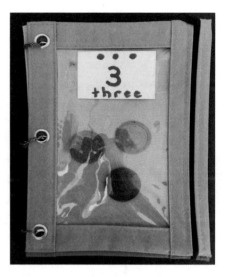

For children who need a challenge, put random amounts of objects in each pocket and leave off the sticky notes. Encourage the children to examine the closed pockets, estimate how many items are in each pocket, and then take out the objects and count to confirm.

For a greater challenge, write simple addition facts on sticky notes and put them on the pencil pockets. Ask the children to make sets of objects in the pockets that represent the addition facts and then count the objects to verify how many in all.

Count at School Book

Learning Opportunities

Counting
Writing numerals
Small-motor skills

Materials

School-supply catalog or photographs of common classroom objects
Construction paper
Book rings
Scissors
Glue
Erasable and regular markers
Paper towels
Clear sheet protectors

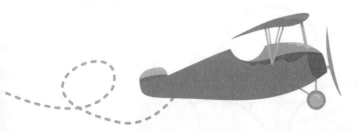

What to Do

Cut out photos of objects you find in your classroom (for example, a boy, a girl, a table, a teacher, an easel, an electronic device, and so on), and glue each photo onto a piece of construction paper. At the top of each page, write "How many [objects]?" Leave a blank line at the bottom of the page. Laminate or place the pages in sheet protectors and put them together with book rings to make a book.

Create several of these books, and distribute them to the children. Ask the children to walk around the room, look at the photos of the objects, count the number of each object in the classroom, and write their answers on the lines with an erasable marker. After they have finished, they can erase their answers with paper towels. Don't worry if the children write the wrong number or write a numeral incorrectly (backward, for example). It's the process of having them count and feel as if they are mathematicians that's important.

Note: Put in pictures of several things you don't have in your classroom, such as a lion or pirate, to help the children understand the concept of *zero*.

For outside fun, make a similar book with pictures of objects on the playground such as trees, swings, riding toys, and so on. Bring the book outside, and ask the children to count the numbers of objects they see outside.

Using My "Own" Cell Phone

Learning Opportunities

Number recognition
Letter recognition
Large-motor skills
Sight words

Materials

Shower curtain liner
Permanent marker
Beanbags
Fly swatter
Card stock
Scissors
Markers

What to Do

Cut a shower curtain liner in half vertically, and draw the keys of a cell phone on the curtain with a permanent marker. Lay the "cell phone" on the floor. Invite each child to throw a beanbag onto a number on the cell phone, identify the number, and then do that number of jumping jacks. For a greater challenge, ask the children to throw two beanbags onto two numbers on the phone and then add up the numbers.

Children can also use a fly swatter to "swat" out their phone numbers. Ask them if they can swat out their names or sight words.

After playing with the giant cell phone, give the children their own paper cell phones. Copy the phone pattern on card stock, and ask the children to cut out individual cell phones. Encourage them to decorate the backs of the phones to make their own "cases." Laminate the phones after the children cut them out so the phones last longer. Challenge the children to identify numbers and letters, spell their names, and so on, on their phones.

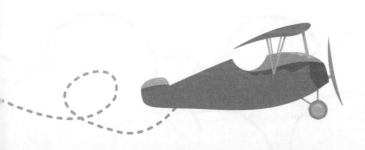

Flippers

Learning Opportunities

Subitizing
Number recognition

Materials

Spatula
Corrugated cardboard or fun foam
Markers
Scissors

What to Do

Draw and then cut out 3 ½-inch circles from cardboard or fun foam. Draw dots on one side of the circles, and write the matching numerals on the backs of the circles. Place the circles with the dots facing up on the floor or a table. Ask the children to identify the number of dots on each circle and then flip it over with the spatula to self-check.

For a greater challenge, write math questions on the fronts of the circles and the answers on the backs, so that the children can practice math facts.

Number Grid Game

Learning Opportunities

Number recognition
Subitizing

Materials

Number grid, 1 per child
1 die
Crayons

What to Do

Give each child a number grid with the numerals 1–6. Ask the children to take turns rolling the die and then coloring in a box on the grid with that number. After playing the game, ask the children which number "won" (had the most boxes colored in).

For a challenge, create number grids with the numerals 2–12 and give children two dice that they roll and then add up before coloring in the boxes on the grid.

Addition Mat

Learning Opportunities

Addition
Number recognition

Materials

12" squares of poster board, 1 for each child
Markers
Ruler
Counters (paper clips, buttons, pennies, and so on)

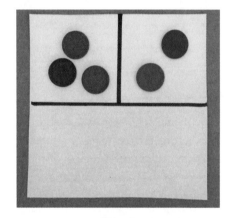

What to Do

Draw lines on the poster board squares similar to the ones shown in the picture. Explain to the children that the line in the middle is like the equals sign in an equation. What is on the top has to equal (or be the same as) what is on the bottom. Demonstrate how to make a set in the top left section and a set in the top right section, and then ask the children to count the objects in each square. Tell them to pull down the objects into the bottom section and then count how many altogether. You can demonstrate subtraction by removing objects from the mat, then counting how many are left.

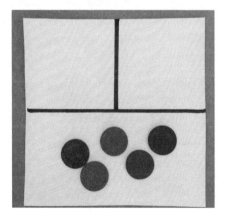

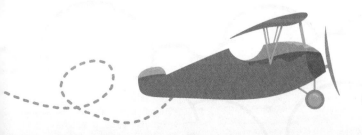

For additional support, encourage each child to do this with a friend and take turns.

For a greater challenge, give the children flash cards to work out on the addition mats.

For even more fun, have the children use divided plates in a similar manner.

Estimate and Check

Learning Opportunities

Estimating

Counting

Materials

5 ziplock bags

Counters (paper clips, bears, buttons, pennies, and so on)

Marker

Recording sheets

Pencils

What to Do

Label the ziplock bags *A, B, C, D,* and *E*. Fill each bag with 1–10 counters. Prepare recording sheets with spaces to record estimates (guesses) and answers. Give each child (or pairs or groups) one bag at a time. Ask her to estimate the number of items in the bag and write it on the corresponding line on the recording sheet. After she has estimated the number of items, ask her to open the bag, count the objects, and write the answer on the corresponding line on the recording sheet. Did she guess more, fewer, or an equal number?

For even more fun, engage children daily in problem solving by asking them questions such as "Do we have enough chairs for everyone?" "Are there extra snacks today?" and "Do we need more pencils?"

Longer and Shorter

Learning Opportunities

Measuring

Comparisons

Materials

5 connecting cubes per child

Basket of classroom objects (pencil, crayon, book, eraser, block, and so on)

6-inch piece of string or yarn, 1 per child

What to Do

Ask the children to measure the different items in the basket with the five connecting cubes, and identify if the items are *longer* or *shorter* than the five cubes. For more fun, encourage the children to walk around the room and compare objects to the length of their cubes by using the words *longer* and *shorter*. Ask them to use a whisper voice and only use the words *longer* and *shorter*.

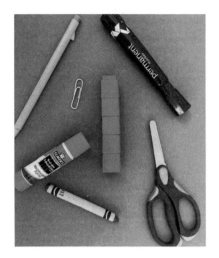

Take the fun outside by giving children 6-inch pieces of string or yarn. Ask them to walk around the playground and identify objects that are *longer* or *shorter* than their string.

Button Counters

Learning Opportunities

Measuring
Counting

Materials

Clear packaging tape
10 buttons
Basket with classroom objects (crayon, glue stick, child-safe scissors, wooden block, and so on)
Scissors

What to Do

Place a 14-inch piece of packaging tape sticky-side up on a table. Put ten buttons end to end in the middle of the tape. Fold the top of the tape down to cover half the buttons, fold the bottom up to cover the other half, and then seal the tape. Trim off the ends. Ask the children to take objects from the basket and then measure the objects with their button counters. Ask them how many buttons long each object is.

For a challenge, encourage the children to put their button counters together and measure larger classroom objects (table, shelf, rug, and so on) as they count by tens.

Outside, invite the children to use button counters on the playground to measure playground equipment and natural objects.

> Snack-time counting: Did you know that Cheez-It crackers are 1-inch squares? Children can place the crackers by objects and count to measure. Then they can eat the crackers for snack!

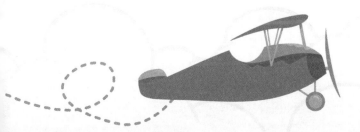

Seriation Snakes

Learning Opportunities

Comparisons
Measuring

Materials

Ribbon or yarn
Scissors

What to Do

Cut yarn or ribbon into five graduated pieces that range from 2 to 10 inches long. Ask the children to put them in order from shortest to longest. Mix up the pieces and ask the children to arrange them from longest to shortest.

For a greater challenge, give children playdough and ask them to roll the playdough into snakes. Encourage them to arrange the snakes in order by length. Ask, "Which one is longest? Which one is shortest?" Challenge the children to create two snakes that are the same length.

Outside, ask children to order rocks, sticks, and other natural objects from shortest to longest.

Fishing for Shapes

Learning Opportunities

Shape recognition
Eye-hand coordination

Materials

Construction paper or fun foam
Glue
Scissors
Paper clips or metal brad fastener
Shapes (triangles, squares, circles, rectangles, and so on) cut from different colors of construction paper
12-inch stick or cardboard roller from a pants hanger
20-inch piece of string
Magnet
Large plastic hoop or masking tape

What to Do

Draw and then cut fish from construction paper or fun foam. Glue a different shape to each fish. Attach a paper clip or brad fastener for the eye of each fish. Tie one end of the string to the stick and the other end to the magnet to make a "fishing pole." Place a large plastic hoop on the floor for the "pond," or make a circle on the floor with masking tape. Place the fish inside the hoop or circle, and demonstrate how to catch one by attaching the magnet to the eye of the fish. Invite the children to take turns to catch a fish and identify the shape.

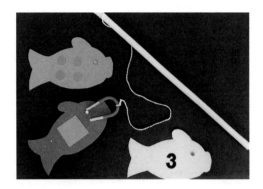

For more fun, use this game to reinforce other skills by replacing the shapes with children's names, colors, letters, numbers, and sight words.

Take the fun outside by making a "pond" on the playground with a large plastic hoop. Put the fish in the pond, and give the children the "fishing pole" to catch the fish.

Shape Town

Learning Opportunities

Shape recognition
Identifying shapes
Sorting
Small-motor skills

Materials

Objects from home that are different shapes (square, triangle, circle, rectangle)
Large, shallow storage container or tub

What to Do

Invite the children to bring items from home that are shapes you are working on (for example, square, triangle, circle, rectangle). Alternatively, ask the children to go on a shape hunt and find objects that match those shapes in the classroom. Place the items in the container and call it Shape Town. Ask the children to match like shapes and then identify the shapes. They can also use the shapes to build their own shape sculptures.

For a challenge, introduce 3-D shapes and place them in Shape Town.

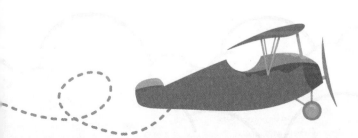

For even more fun, cut geometric shapes out of construction paper and let the children use them to make collages. Can they arrange them to look like an object or animal?

Outside, look for shapes on the playground or take a nature walk and identify shapes.

Mystery Shapes

Learning Opportunities

Shape recognition
Sensorimotor skills

Materials

4 paper lunch bags
Items in specific shapes (square, triangle, rectangle, circle)
Construction paper cut into matching shapes (square, triangle, rectangle, circle)

What to Do

Put each item in a different bag, and place the four construction-paper shapes on the table. Ask the children to reach into each bag, feel a shape, and match it with the similar shape on the table. After the children have sorted the shapes, encourage them to check to see if they are correct. When they match an item with a shape, ask them how they knew this was a match. Put the shapes back in the bags and play the game again. After repeating the game several times, children will become better at noticing the different attributes of the shapes.

For children who need additional support, put foam or wooden shapes in the bags so it will be easier for them to feel the shapes and identify the shapes' different attributes.

For a greater challenge, put all the different shapes in one bag. Ask each child to choose one shape at a time, identify it, and then remove it from the bag to self-check.

For even more fun, play this game with 3-D shapes, such as a cube, a triangular prism, a rectangular prism, and a sphere.

Place Value

Learning Opportunities

Place value
Counting
Small-motor skills

Materials

Craft sticks
Rubber bands
File folder
Marker

What to Do

Draw a line down the middle fold of a file folder. Write *Tens* on the left side and *Ones* on the right side. Ask the children to gather a set of ten craft sticks, bind it with a rubber band, and place that bundle under *Tens*. Then ask the children to add one craft stick at a time under *Ones* until they make another set of ten, then bind that set of sticks with a rubber band. Encourage the children to count the bundles by tens and then continue adding one stick at a time and counting on.

For additional support, provide children with enough sticks so that they can count by ones as high as they can go.

For a greater challenge, ask children to count by tens to 100 using the bundles. Put 10 bundles of 10 sticks together to make 100.

Writing Numerals

Learning Opportunities

Writing numerals
Number recognition
Small-motor skills

Materials

School glue
Poster board or heavy paper
Scissors
Markers
Copy paper cut in half
Old crayons with the paper removed
Chalk

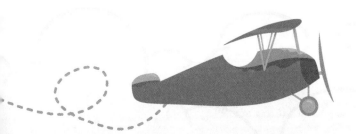

What to Do

Cut the poster board or heavy paper into 6" x 4" rectangles. Write a numeral on each rectangle using dots of glue, and let the glue dry completely. Ask the children to trace over the numerals with their fingers as they say the number words. Next, have them place half sheets of paper on top of the numerals and rub over the dots with the sides of the crayons. Ask them to connect the dots with crayons and repeat the number words one more time.

Hint: Put a green dot where they begin writing the numeral and a red dot where they should end.

Take the fun outside by using chalk to make a hopscotch game board on a paved surface. Write numerals in the sections, and ask the children to hop on the numerals as they count.

Science Center

"The creation of something new is not accomplished by the intellect but by the play instinct acting from inner necessity."

—Carl Jung, psychiatrist

In the science center, children are able to explore, observe, solve problems, make decisions, develop concepts about science and nature, improve language, interact socially, and develop sensory skills. Children are naturally curious about the world around them. Support this curiosity by providing opportunities—and tools to use—to investigate how the world and the things in it work.

Research tells us that children will be more engaged in scientific explorations if their teachers model how to use science tools, such as magnifying glasses, measuring tape, thermometers, and balance scales (Nayfield, Gelman, and Brenneman, 2011). Show your interest and excitement in exploring, and the children will follow your example.

Materials for the Science Center

Shelves, tables	Pictures and posters	Nature exhibits (collections of rocks, shells, bones, insects, and so on)
Lab coats	Thermometer	
Safety goggles	Flashlight	Field guides
Magnifying glasses	Feely box	Clipboard, paper, pencils
Magnets	Sensory materials	Planting area to grow sprouts, flowers, herbs, and so on
Plants	Terrarium	
Prism	Models (dinosaurs, insects)	
Aquarium		
Balance scale	Mirror	
Science books, magazines	Seeds, leaves, flowers, feathers	

Tip: Rotate natural items to reflect the season and what is in your environment.

I Know a Scientist

Learning Opportunities

Singing
Vocabulary
Pretend play

Materials

Old white dress shirt, 1 per child
Scissors
Marker

What to Do

To find enough old shirts, ask families to send these in, or purchase them at a thrift store. Cut the ends of the sleeves off to fit children's arms, and write "Dr. [child's name]" on the pocket of each shirt. Whenever you do a science-related activity in your class, encourage the children to put on their lab coats like real scientists. Relate how they can observe, make hypotheses, predict, experiment, do research, and record data just like real scientists. Instilling a love of science and a belief that "I am a scientist" is a powerful attitude to plant in young children.

Teach children this song, sung to the tune of "I Had a Little Turtle":

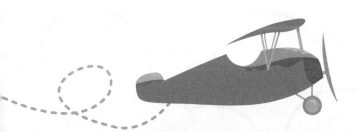

I Know a Scientist

I know a scientist, (Hold up index finger.)

And you can be one, too! (Point with index finger.)

Here's the scientific method

So you'll know what to do.

First, you find a question. (Hold up one finger.)

Just take a look around. (Pretend to look around.)

What is it that you want to know?

Now you write it down.

Next you make a guess. (Hold up two fingers.)

It's called a hypothesis

About what will happen

When you do your tests.

Now experiment, (Hold up three fingers)

Observe it. Write it, too. (Hold up four fingers.)

You'll need lots of data

To show your guess is true.

Draw your conclusions. (Hold up five fingers.)

Look into any doubts.

Then tell everybody

What you've found out!

For even more fun, introduce the children to terms for various categories of science. For example, when studying insects, refer to the children as *entomologists*, or when studying the weather, call them *meteorologists*. Consider incorporating safety goggles into your scientific explorations. Invite guest speakers to share their expertise on topics that interest the children.

Naturalist Kits

Learning Opportunities

Observation
Pretend play
Sorting and classifying

Materials

Plastic container with a handle, such as a small bucket
Paper-towel rolls
Scissors
Tape
Hole punch
String
Magnifying glasses
Field guides
Tweezers
Ziplock bags for collecting specimens
Paper
Pencils

What to Do

Make a naturalist kit for each child by recycling a plastic container with a handle, such as a small bucket. Add a magnifying glass, field guide, tweezers, ziplock bags for collecting specimens, paper, pencil, and so on to the buckets.

Make binoculars by cutting a cardboard paper-towel roll in half. Tape the halves together and hole punch at the top. Loop a piece of string through the holes, and tie it long enough to go around a child's neck and hang down to his chest, so the child can easily take the binoculars on and off.

Talk to the children about what naturalists do, and invite them to be naturalists. Pair children, and let them take turns playing "naturalist" on the playground with their naturalist kits.

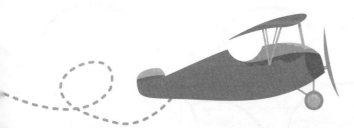

Science Journal

Learning Opportunities

Recording data
Writing skills
Cooperation

Materials

5 sheets of white paper per journal
Rubber bands
Hole punch
Craft sticks approximately 8 inches long
Note: This list of materials makes one journal; make a journal for each child.

What to Do

Fold the paper in half. Make two holes on the creased edge, about 2 inches from each end. Put a rubber band through one hole with the small part of the loop outside the crease, on the "spine." Insert one end of the stick in the loop. Hold the stick and rubber band in place as you stretch the rubber band and put the other end of the rubber band through the other hole. Attach the other end of the stick through that loop, so that the craft stick forms a support for the spine of the journal. Encourage the children to use these journals to record data, write about experiments, or draw observations.

Let children take their science journals home once a week and explain what they are studying to their families. Invite families to write their "comments and compliments" in the journals.

Color Discs

Learning Opportunities

Observing
Experimenting
Communication skills
Recognizing primary and secondary colors

Materials

6 paper plates
Scissors
Stapler
Red, yellow, and blue cellophane or acetate

What to Do

Using a paper plate as a pattern, cut circles out of the cellophane or acetate. (Clear report covers work well.) Cut the centers out of the plates. Staple a different color of cellophane in between each pair of paper plate rims. Encourage the children to experiment by looking through each color and then by putting two colors together and holding them up to the light.

Explain to the children that red, yellow, and blue are primary colors. When you put the primary colors together, you get the secondary colors of green, orange, and purple. Encourage the children to name the two colors they put together (primary colors) and the color that they create (secondary color).

For more fun, make individual necklaces for each child using two primary colors of cellophane. Cut a square or circle of each color. Punch holes in the squares/circles and insert a piece of string or yarn long enough to fit comfortably over the children's heads.

Out on the playground, invite the children to experiment with the color paddles. Can they make different colored "lights" on the sidewalk by holding the paddles so that the sun shines through them?

Color Mixing

Learning Opportunities

Experimenting
Observing
Recognizing primary and
secondary colors
Small-motor skills

Materials

Clear cups
Water
Red, blue, and yellow food
coloring
Paper towels
Eyedroppers

What to Do

Prepare three cups of water with red, blue, and yellow food coloring. Encourage the children to use the eyedroppers to drop colored water to create secondary colors on paper towels.

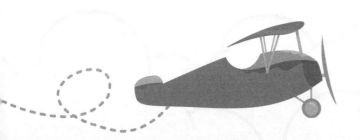

For even more fun, give each child two small balls of different primary-color playdough. (Make the lighter-color ball a little bigger so the darker color doesn't dominate.) Encourage the children to pinch off a piece of their playdough, get a pinch of playdough from a friend with a different color, and then see what happens when they knead them together.

Nature Center

Learning Opportunities

Observing
Counting
Sorting
Scribbling and drawing
Emergent writing

Materials

Plastic tub
Natural items, such as leaves, rocks, shells, pinecones, sticks, and nuts
Magnifying glasses
Clipboards
Pencils
Paper
Field guides on leaves, rocks, shells, and so on

What to Do

Put the natural objects in the tub. Children can use them for free exploration as well as for developing different skills, such as sorting by color, texture, or another characteristic; counting, seriating by size or weight, observing, and emerging writing. Rotate the objects for different seasons.

For outside fun, provide the children with magnifying glasses, field guides, clipboards, and pencils and paper so they can explore with these items on the playground.

Living and Nonliving Things

Learning Opportunities

Asking questions
Classifying
Sorting

Materials

Living items (bits of grass, acorns, dandelions and other plants, seeds, and so on)
Nonliving items (water bottle, crayons, pencils, toys, stuffed animals, rocks, and so on)

What to Do

Bring in items for the children to sort into groups of living and nonliving things. Explain to the children that living things are alive now or once were alive and that nonliving things are not, and never were, alive.

Describe the characteristics of living things: they need nutrients and water, they grow and move, they reproduce, and they breathe. Explain that people, animals, and plants breathe in a process called *respiration*. Plants don't have lungs or a blood stream like animals do, but they use their leaves and roots to breathe in carbon dioxide and turn it into oxygen that people and animals need to breathe.

Mix all the living and nonliving items together, and put them on a table. Encourage the children to ask each other the following questions to determine if each item is living or nonliving and to sort the items into two piles:

- Does it eat?
- Does it breathe?
- Does it grow?
- Does it *reproduce* (make new living things)?

Monitor the children's sorting, and when they are finished, encourage them to tell you how they know each item belongs in the category where they sorted it.

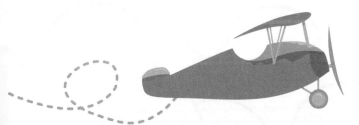

Magic Mirror

Learning Opportunities

Observing
Experimenting

Materials

Unbreakable (child-safe) hand mirrors
Magazines or catalogs
Scissors
Glue
File folders

What to Do

Cut small pictures from magazines or catalogs in half, and glue one-half of each picture to a file folder. Ask the children to place the hand mirrors next to each picture to make the other half of the image.

For a greater challenge, ask the children to write their names and then hold the mirrors next to them. What happened to their names?

Discovery Bottles

Discovery bottles are open-ended materials that provide children with lots of hands-on exploration and opportunities for observation. They are inexpensive, simple to make, and a great way to model reusing materials in new ways. Just remember to glue the lids on, because the children might be tempted to do a little too much exploration!

For a home-school connection, invite the children to create discovery bottles at home with their families. Provide directions for one or more of the bottles from this book, or encourage each family to "invent" their own bottle. Then, the children can bring in their bottles to share with their classmates.

Muddy Water Bottle

Learning Opportunities

Observing
Experimenting
Comparisons
Using recyclable materials

Materials

Plastic bottle
Dirt
Glue
Water

What to Do

Put half a cup of dirt in the bottom of the bottle. Fill two-thirds of the bottle with water. Glue on the lid. Encourage the children to shake the bottle and observe the dirt as it settles to the bottom.

For even more fun, add sand, peat moss, potting soil, or gravel to bottles of water. Ask the children to compare what happens when they shake the different bottles. Which one settles first? Which one is the slowest to settle?

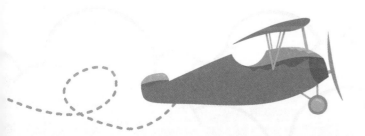

Beach Bottle

Learning Opportunities

Observing
Experimenting
Using recyclable materials

Materials

Plastic bottle
Sand
Water
Blue food coloring
Small shells
Small balloon
Permanent marker
Glue

What to Do

Rinse the sand until the water runs clear. Put three-fourths of a cup of sand in the bottom of the bottle, and fill the bottle almost to the top with water. Add a drop of blue food coloring and the shells. To make a fish, blow a little air into the balloon and knot it. Draw a face on the balloon with a permanent marker and put it in the bottle. Glue on the lid. Invite the children to move the bottle so the "fish" swims. For even more fun, if you live by the ocean or a large lake, collect sand from different beaches and label each bottle with the name of the beach it came from.

Static Electricity Bottle

Learning Opportunities

Observing
Experimenting
Using recyclable materials

Materials

Plastic bottle
Tissue paper
Glue

What to Do

Tear the tissue paper into little pieces and put the pieces into the bottle. Glue on the lid. Briskly stroke the bottle on the carpet, your hair, or a wool sweater. Ask the children to observe what happens.

For even more fun, cut tissue paper into the shape of small butterflies or birds. When you move the bottle on the carpet, your hair, or a wool sweater, the butterflies or birds will look as if they are flying.

Magnetic Bottle

Learning Opportunities

Observing
Experimenting
Using recyclable materials

Materials

Plastic bottle
Shredded paper
18-inch piece of string
Magnet
Small objects magnets will attract (pins, nails, paper clips, toys, and so on)
Glue

What to Do

Fill two-thirds of the bottle with shredded paper. Put in the different objects and then glue on the lid. Tie one end of the string to the neck of the bottle and tie the magnet to the other end of the string. Invite the children to move the magnet along the side of the bottle to attract the objects.

For even more fun, put paper clips in a bottle and fill it with water. Encourage the children to move the magnet along the side of the bottle to attract the paper clips.

Wave Bottle

Learning Opportunities

Observing
Experimenting
Using recyclable materials

Materials

Plastic bottle
Food coloring
Baby oil
Glue

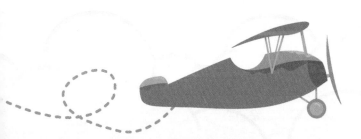

What to Do

Fill two-thirds of the bottle with water. Add several drops of food coloring. Fill the bottle to the top with the oil, and then glue on the lid. Ask the children to slowly move the bottle on its side to create waves. Encourage them to shake up the bottle and then observe as the oil and water separate.

Mystery Sound

Learning Opportunities

Observing
Experimenting
Predicting
Using recyclable materials

Materials

Several plastic bottles
Old socks
Pebbles
Paper clips
Sand
Counting bears

What to Do

Fill each bottle with a half cup of one of the filler items listed above, and replace the lids. Place each bottle in an old sock. Ask the children to shake the bottles and try to identify what is inside each bottle. Let them remove the bottles from the socks to verify their predictions. For even more fun, make two bottles of each item. Mix up the bottles, and then challenge children to match up ones with the same sound.

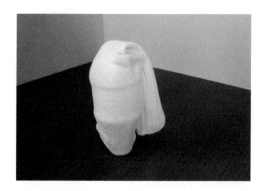

Bubble Bottle

Learning Opportunities

Observing
Experimenting
Using recyclable materials

Materials

Plastic bottle
Dish detergent
Food coloring
Water
Glue

What to Do

Put a half-cup of water in the bottle. Add a drop of detergent and a drop of food coloring. Glue on the lid. Invite the children to shake the bottle and observe. Ask them to observe what happens to the bubbles if the bottle sits for a while.

For even more fun, use shampoo and different types of detergent to make several bubble bottles. Use a permanent marker to write each bottle's main ingredient on the outside of the bottle. Ask the children to shake the bottles and find out which one makes the most bubbles.

I Spy Bottle

Learning Opportunities

Observing
Experimenting
Using recyclable materials
Prewriting skills

Materials

Plastic bottle
Sand or salt
5–10 small toys or objects (crayon, eraser, hairbow, penny, counting bear, and so on)
Paper
Markers or crayons
Glue

What to Do

Fill two-thirds of the bottle with sand or salt. Drop the toys and other items into the bottle and glue on the lid. Shake to hide the objects. Ask the children to shake the bottle. How many things can the children "spy" in the bottle? Encourage them to draw pictures or write down all of the objects that they see. For the different seasons and holidays, consider making bottles with toys and other small objects that are relevant.

Imagination Station

Learning Opportunities

Creativity
Imagination
Independence
Experimenting
Self-expression
Social skills

Materials

Crayons, markers, colored pencils, and pens
Tape
Glue
Hole punches
Child-safe scissors
String
Paper-towel tubes
Cardboard
Paper
Shoe boxes, tissue boxes, and oatmeal boxes
Toothpicks
Straws
Cotton balls
Cotton swabs
Wallpaper sample books
Aluminum foil
Clay

What to Do

Tell the children that they are inventors! Every day, they imagine and create different things as they play. This activity gives them the chance to work together and be creative. With the children, brainstorm a list of objects you have seen them create while playing, such as car ramps, garages for toy cars, a zoo, doll houses, a mailbox for special notes, and so on. Encourage them to use the materials in the Imagination Station to invent something.

For even more fun, hold an Imagination Celebration when all of the inventions are completed, so the children can look at their friends' projects and share what they made. Take pictures of the creations for a class book.

What's in the Egg? Flip Book

Learning Opportunities

Predicting
Small-motor skills
Creativity

Materials

Paper
Scissors
Pencils or crayons

What to Do

Fold the paper in half. (Some call this making a "hot dog" fold.) Fold the paper in half again. (Some call this a "hamburger" fold.) Fold the paper in half again. (Some call this making a "juice box" fold.) Open and cut the crease in the middle fold. Fold in half to make four little flaps. Ask the children to draw four eggs, one on the front of each flap. Then ask them to open the flaps and draw four different things that might come from an egg. Tell the children to hold the book up to the light to see their little critters inside the eggs.

Invite them to share their egg flip books with each other and try to guess what's inside the eggs.

Playing with Water

Many children love playing with water, exploring how it moves and feels. Water provides lots of learning opportunities for discovery and vocabulary growth. Invite the children you teach to learn all about water!

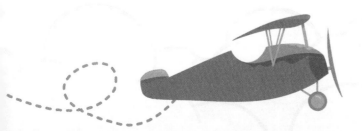

What Is Water?

Learning Opportunities

Observing
Predicting
Vocabulary

Materials

Clear containers in different sizes (tall, short, round, square, and so on)
Glass
Water
Small cups

What to Do

Place a glass of water and several clear containers on a table. Hold up the glass of water. Ask the children what it is, and encourage them to describe water. Introduce vocabulary words such as *fluid*, *transparent*, *odorless*, and *tasteless*. Ask the children, "What will happen if I pour the water into this tall glass? What will happen if I pour the water into this square container?" Pour the water into the different containers. Summarize by saying that water is *fluid* and takes the shape of the container.

Give each child a small cup of water. Encourage the children to see what they can find out about water by observing it. Ask, for example:

- What color is it? Note that water doesn't have any color and we can see through it, so we say it is *transparent*.
- Does it have a smell? Explain to the children that water is *odorless* because it doesn't usually smell. If it does have a smell, ask them to describe it.
- Does it make a sound? Ask them to describe the sound that water makes.
- What shape is it? Explain that it takes the shape of whatever container it is in, so we say that it is *fluid*. Encourage the children to drink the water. Ask how it tastes. Affirm that water is indeed *tasteless*.
- Invite them to touch the water. Ask them to describe how it feels.

Our Bodies Need Water

Learning Opportunities

Vocabulary
Predicting
Sorting
Recording data
Counting

Materials

Dry-erase board
Chart paper
Markers

What to Do

On the chart paper, make a table with four columns. Label the columns *one-fourth*, *two-fourths*, *three-fourths*, and *four-fourths*.

Explain to the children that living things need water to help their bodies function. Ask the children to predict how much of their bodies is water. Draw a square on the dry-erase board, and divide it into fourth smaller squares. Count the fourths with the children: one, two, three, four. Color in one-fourth of the square, and tell them that this represents *one-fourth*. (Note: Don't worry about whether the children understand fractions. The goal of this activity is expose them to the concept of fractions while exploring one of the differences between living and nonliving things.) Ask, "Who thinks their body is one-fourth water? Count the number of children who think so, and make that number of tally marks on the table in the *one-fourth* column, counting aloud as you do.

Color in another section of the square. Ask, "Who thinks their body is two-fourths water?" Count the number of children who think so, and make that number of tally marks number on the table in the *two-fourths* column, counting aloud as you do.

Color in another section. Ask, "Who thinks their body is three-fourths water?" Count the number of children who think so, and make that number of marks on the table in the *three-fourths* column, counting aloud as you do.

Color in the last section. Ask, "Who thinks their body is four-fourths water?" (Explain that this means entirely made of water.) Count the number of children who think so, and write this number on the table in the *four-fourths* column, counting aloud as you do. Look at the data on the chart and ask the children which column has the most marks.

Then, tell the children that their bodies are composed of three-fourths water! That's a lot of water! Their bodies need to take in (drink) water to stay healthy. Ask them what other living things need water. They may say plants, animals, and people. Ask them whether some nonliving things, such as rocks, plastic toys, and shovels, need water. Remind them that living things need water, but nonliving things do not need water.

For more fun, do a water web on the board or a large piece of paper. Write *water* in the middle, and then ask the children to tell you some ways we use water. They may say swimming, drinking, bathing, splashing, watering plants, brushing their teeth, and so on.

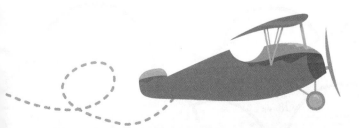

Absorb or Repel

Learning Opportunities

Observing
Predicting
Recording data
Small-motor skills

Materials

Small cups
Water
Eyedroppers
Materials that will absorb water, such as tissue, cotton balls, paper towels, and fabric
Materials that will repel water, such as wax paper, aluminum foil, a plastic plate, Styrofoam, and blocks
Paper
Markers
Photos or samples of the materials to be tested
Glue
Pencils

What to Do

Create an observation sheet with three columns. In the first column, from top to bottom, glue a picture or sample of each material the children will test. Write *absorb* as the heading for the second column and *repel* as the heading for the third column. Make enough copies for each child to have one.

With the children, introduce the vocabulary words *absorb* and *repel*. Tell them that when something absorbs water, it takes the water in. When something repels water, the water just rolls right off.

Give each child an observation sheet. Point to the pictures or samples in the first column, and tell them that each one is a material they get to test in a water experiment. Point to the other two columns and read the headings. Explain that they will use the observation sheet to predict whether the different materials will absorb or repel the water.

Ask them to look at each material and predict whether it will absorb (take in) water or repel (not take in) water. They can write *yes* or *Y* or simply make a check mark in the appropriate column for each item.

Next, let the children test each material by dipping an eyedropper into a cup of water, then dropping water on the material. If their prediction for that material was correct, they can circle the check mark or *Y* or *yes*.

Talk with them about the results of their experiments. Ask them which materials absorb water and which repel water. Ask them what they think makes a material absorb water. Ask them what they think makes a material repel water.

Sink or Float?

Learning Opportunities

Observing
Predicting
Recording results
Small-motor skills
Prewriting skills

Materials

Small tub of water
Objects that will float, such as paper towel pieces, paper clips, ground pepper
Objects that will sink, such as a large block, a large plastic toy, a rock, a ball of clay
Observation sheet, 1 per child
Pencils
Marker

What to Do

Create an observation sheet with a three-column grid. Leave the first column blank. Write *sink* as the heading for the second column and *float* as the heading for the third column. Make enough copies for each child to have one.

With the children, introduce the vocabulary words *sink* and *float*. Tell them that when something sinks, it drops to the bottom of the container of water. When something floats, it stays on the surface of the water.

Give each child an observation sheet. In the first column, ask them to write the name or draw a picture of an object they will test. Then they can make a check mark in the column for their prediction: sink or float.

Next, let the children predict and test each material by placing the objects in the water. Were their predictions correct? Have the children circle the marks that show correct predictions.

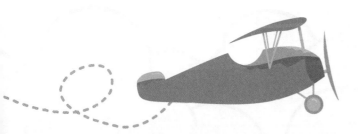

Block Center

> "We don't stop playing because we grow old;
> we grow old because we stop playing."
> —George Bernard Shaw, playwright

Blocks are a fabulous tool for learning. Playing and exploring with blocks helps children develop concepts of number, size, shape, space, and weight. Blocks also encourage children's imagination and self-confidence and improve their language, social, and motor skills. Persisting through trial and error, children will build increasingly complex structures (Hanline, Milton, and Phelps, 2001). All you have to do is watch children playing in the block center and you'll observe their pleasure and personal satisfaction.

Create your classroom's block center on a carpeted area to keep down the noise, and add shelves to contain the materials. Consider providing children with a camera to take pictures of their structures to share with their families. For specific learning activities with blocks, place the relevant materials in tubs.

Three simple rules children should follow in the block center:

1. Build only as tall as you are.
2. Knock down only what you build.
3. Put the blocks away when you are finished.

The Possibilities of Play

Materials for the Block Center

Unit blocks of various shapes and sizes

Cardboard boxes

Alphabet blocks

Blocks with the children's faces on them

Wooden dollhouse and furniture

Wooden barn and animals

Plastic dinosaurs and animals

Toy train set, boats, airplanes

Small dolls or action figures

Plastic bins or boxes for accessories

Wooden cars and trucks

Toy street signs

Bristle blocks

Lincoln Logs

Construction hats, carpenter's apron, blueprints

Engineer planning book

Maps

Paper

Pencils

Pattern blocks

Engineer Planning Book

Learning Opportunities

Engineering skills
Spatial awareness
Small-motor skills
Creativity

Materials

Spiral notebook
Pencils

What to Do

Write "Engineer Planning Book" on the cover of the notebook. Explain to the children that engineers draw plans and then try to build their designs. Place the book in the block center along with a pencil. Encourage the children to draw their ideas in the book and then try to build them.

For a greater challenge, make individual engineer planning books for each child to use in the block center by stapling several sheets of white paper together. Encourage the children to decorate and use their engineer planning books in the center. They can take photos of their constructions, too, and add them to their planning books as a record of their creations.

Block Book

Learning Opportunities

Visual skills
Small-motor skills
Spatial awareness

Materials

File folders
Construction paper
Glue

What to Do

Cut 1" x 1" squares and 2" x 1" rectangles out of construction paper to represent unit blocks. Arrange these to make structures similar to the ones shown in the photos, and glue them to file folders. Punch holes in the file folders and bind them together to make a book. Place the book in the block center, and challenge the children to look at the designs and then make them with the blocks.

For an extra challenge, ask the children to look at a design and then turn the book over and make the design from memory.

For younger children and children who need extra support, make a counting book with different amounts of blocks for them to reproduce.

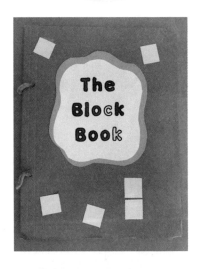

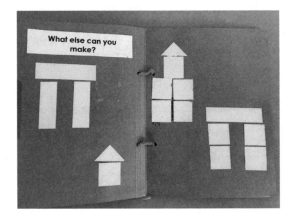

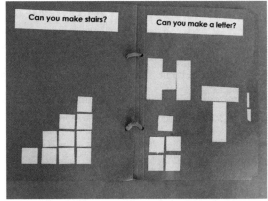

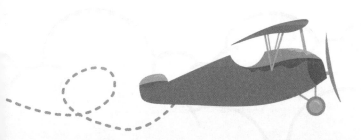

I Can Build . . . Book

Learning Opportunities

Engineering skills
Eye-hand coordination
Small-motor skills

Materials

Paper
Card stock or manila folders
Glue
Hole punch
Yarn or book rings
Images of structures (from old
magazines or found online)

What to Do

Create a book filled with images of structures to inspire the children. You could include images of bridges, buildings, houses, barns, playgrounds, zoos, castles—anything that they could try to build. Glue the images to paper, label each image, and attach these pages to file folders or card stock. Punch holes down one side of the folders, and bind them together with yarn or book rings. Write the title *I Can Build . . .* on the cover, and put the book in the block center to inspire the children.

Encourage the children to build some of the structures and then take pictures of their creations.

For a greater challenge, encourage the children to choose their own pictures of buildings from magazines and newspapers and then try to create them with blocks.

For even more fun, provide toy hard hats for the children to wear as they build.

Green Construction

Learning Opportunities

Engineering skills
Using recyclable materials
Creativity

Materials

Paper grocery bags
Empty cardboard food boxes
Newspaper
Packing tape

What to Do

Ask families to save empty cardboard food boxes for a week. Suggest that they fill up a paper grocery bag with the boxes and bring them in. Invite the children to work together to wad up newspaper and stuff it in the boxes. Help them tape the boxes shut. Encourage the children to use these boxes for building walls, forts, houses, and other large structures inside the classroom as well as outside on the playground.

For a challenge, ask the children to sort the boxes by color, size, or content.

City Designs

Learning Opportunities

Environmental print
Small-motor skills
Creativity

Materials

Store and restaurant logos
Photos of your school and community
Packing tape
Wooden blocks of different sizes
Paper
Markers

What to Do

Find store and restaurant logos on the internet, and then print them and cut them out. Tape the logos to blocks with clear packing tape. Tape pictures of your school, post office, and other places in your community to other blocks. Encourage the children to design a city with the blocks.

For a greater challenge, give the children paper, markers, and tape and let them make their own signs that they tape to blocks for buildings.

For even more fun, walk around your school and community and take pictures of the children's favorite places. Make copies of the pictures and tape them to blocks.

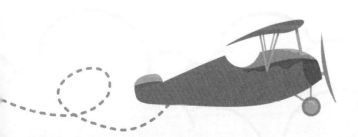

My Friends and Me

Learning Opportunities

Social skills
Oral language

Materials

5" x 7" photo of each child
and teacher
Card stock
Laminator
Binder clips
Scissors
Clear tub or box

What to Do

Take a full-length picture of each child and teacher and print it on card stock. Cut out the pictures and laminate. Attach a binder clip to the bottom so each picture will stand up. Place the pictures in a clear tub or box and store them in the block center. Encourage the children to use the pictures in the block center.

For a greater challenge, invite the children to draw characters from stories. Laminate the characters, cut them out, and attach binder clips so the children can use them to retell the stories.

For even more fun, attach photos of famous people or story characters to paper-towel rolls cut in half. These can be used to prompt storytelling and children's imaginations.

Plates and Cups

Learning Opportunities

Eye-hand coordination
Creativity
Small-motor skills

Materials

Small plastic cups
Dessert-sized paper plates

What to Do

Put out the plates and cups, and invite the children to be builders. Demonstrate how to stack a plate on top of a cup and then add another plate and cup. Show the children how to build a pyramid by placing two cups on a table or the floor and then placing a third on top. You can also demonstrate how to build a pyramid with six cups.

For a greater challenge, ask the children to count how many plates and cups they can stack.

For more fun, offer the children larger cups and dinner-sized plates for building.

Bring the plates and cups outside so the children can build with them on a picnic table on the playground.

Tower Topple

Learning Opportunities

Eye-hand coordination
Social skills

Materials

Unit blocks

What to Do

Play this game with two or more children. Ask the first child to choose a block and place it on the floor. Then ask the second child to choose a block and place it on top of the first block. The third child should then select another block and place it on top of the first two. The game continues as the children try to build as high as they can before the tower topples.

For a greater challenge, encourage the children to estimate how many blocks they can stack. Did they use more or fewer than they estimated?

Take the fun outside by bringing a box of blocks on the playground so children can play the game.

Building Math Concepts with Blocks

Blocks are a great material for children to explore and use to learn math concepts as they play.

Sorting with Blocks

Learning Opportunities

Sorting
Visual matching
Self-help skills

Materials

Wooden blocks of various sizes and shapes
Construction paper
Clear laminating sheets or clear packing tape
Scissors
Marker

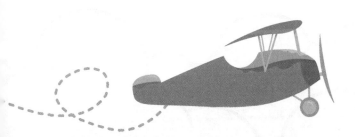

What to Do

Choose one of each wooden block shape and trace around it on the construction paper. Cut it out and use clear packing tape or a laminating sheet to adhere it to your block shelf where the blocks of that shape should be stored. After children are done playing with the blocks, encourage them to sort the blocks and place them in the appropriate spots on the block shelf.

Counting with Blocks

Learning Opportunities

Counting
Number recognition

Materials

Wooden blocks
Dice

What to Do

Ask the children to stack as many blocks as they can and then count them. Encourage them to continue stacking blocks to see if they can add more.

For extra support, give the children one die to roll and ask them to count the number on the die and then stack that many blocks.

For a greater challenge, offer the children two or more dice to roll. Ask them to add the numbers on the dice and then stack that many blocks.

Numerical Order

Learning Opportunities

Counting
Number recognition

Materials

Blocks of the same size
Paper
Markers
Tape
Scissors

The Possibilities of Play

What to Do

Cut paper into ten 2 ½-inch squares. Number each of the squares with a numeral from 1 to 10 and tape each number to a block. Ask the children to put the blocks in order from 1 to 10.

For children who need extra support, use masking tape to make a number line on the floor. Ask the children to match the numbered blocks with the numbers on the number line.

For a challenge, write numbers by tens (10, 20, 30 . . . 100) and then fives (5, 10, 15, 20, and so on) to put these on the blocks. Ask the children to put the blocks in order.

Measuring with Blocks

Learning Opportunities

Measuring
Counting

Materials

Wooden unit blocks

What to Do

Let the children use blocks to measure different objects in the classroom. For example, challenge them to find out how many blocks tall a table is or how many blocks long the room is. Give the children one specific size of block to use when measuring.

For a challenge, let one child lie on the floor so her friends can measure how many square blocks long she is. How many rectangular blocks long is she?

For outside fun, ask the children to take the blocks on the playground and measure natural objects such as branches and bushes.

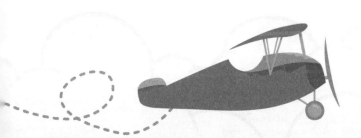

Seriation with Blocks

Learning Opportunities

Sequencing
Visual discrimination

Materials

Unit blocks of different sizes

What to Do

Ask the children to stack unit blocks from largest to smallest, ending with the smallest blocks on top.

For a greater challenge, ask the children to see how many square blocks make a rectangular block. How many small rectangular blocks are equal to the largest rectangular block? How many small squares equal the largest rectangular block? How many small triangles make a square? What other parts can the children put together to make the whole?

Math Symbols and Signs

Learning Opportunities

Addition
Counting
Number recognition

Materials

Square unit blocks
Paper
Numbered blocks
Scissors
Tape
Marker

What to Do

Cut paper into 2 $\frac{1}{2}$-inch squares. Write math symbols on the paper squares, and then tape the symbols onto blocks. Encourage the children to use these with numbered blocks to demonstrate math facts.

For even more fun, put inequality signs on blocks and use for *greater than* and *less than* between numbered blocks.

Building Literacy Skills with Blocks

Blocks are also a great material for children to develop their literacy skills.

Alphabet Recognition with Blocks

Learning Opportunities

Letter recognition
Matching
Phonics

Materials

Square unit blocks
Paper
Tape
Scissors
Marker

What to Do

Cut paper into 2 ½-inch squares, write letters (upper- and lowercase separately) on the paper squares, and then tape the letters onto blocks. Ask the children to match the uppercase letters with the lowercase letters. Encourage the children to name the letters.

Start with ten blocks (five uppercase and five lowercase letters) and increase the number of squares as children become more confident.

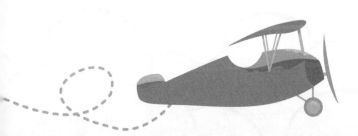

Rhyming Blocks

Learning Opportunities

Rhyming words
Oral language
Matching

Materials

Square unit blocks
Pictures of objects that rhyme
Tape
Scissors

What to Do

Cut out small pictures of objects that rhyme. (You can find free rhyming reproducibles on the internet). Tape the pictures to the blocks. Ask the children to name the object on each block and match it with the rhyming object. Invite the children to think of other words that rhyme with the pictures on the blocks.

Block Names

Learning Opportunities

Letter recognition
Name recognition
Sight words

Materials

Square unit blocks
Paper
Tape
Marker
Scissors

What to Do

Cut paper into 2 ½-inch squares, write the letters of the alphabet on the squares, and then secure the letters with tape to the blocks. Make extra letter blocks for vowels and common consonants, such as M, L, R, S, T, N, and C. Also make extra letter blocks for any letters in the children's names; otherwise, Abbie, Francisco, and Laila will be frustrated! Ask the children to select the letters in their names and then build their names with the blocks.

For children who need additional support, write the children's names on sentence strips so they have a pattern to follow.

For a challenge, ask the children to build their first and last names with the blocks. Invite them to write their names.

For even more of a challenge, ask the children to reproduce sight words with blocks and then write them.

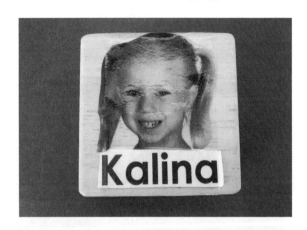

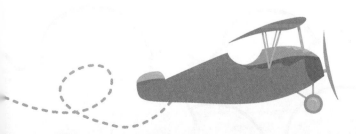

Sequencing with Blocks

Learning Opportunities

Sequencing
Oral language

Materials

Square unit blocks
Sequence graphics
Tape
Scissors

What to Do

Download pictures demonstrating the sequences in nursery rhymes, plant growth, blowing bubbles, and so on. Cut the pictures apart and tape them to the blocks. Ask the children to put the pictures in order and then verbally explain what happens in each sequence; for example, "First, Jack and Jill went up the hill. Then, they got some water in their bucket. Next, Jack fell down . . ."

For an extra challenge, give the children 2 ½-inch squares of paper and ask them to make picture sequences to show what happens in a familiar story.

Phonics Fun with Blocks

Learning Opportunities

Phonics
Matching

Materials

Square unit blocks
Pictures of objects that begin with sounds you want to reinforce
Paper
Marker
Tape
Scissors

What to Do

Cut paper into 2 ½-inch squares. Write the lowercase letters of initial sounds the children are learning on the squares, and tape them to some of the blocks. Tape the pictures to the other blocks. (Old workbooks and worksheets are a great source for these pictures.) Ask the children to match the blocks with initial sounds to the pictures that begin with those same sounds.

The Possibilities of Play

For children who need extra support, partner a child who has mastered this skill with a child who is struggling.

For a challenge, make similar matching games for blends, vowels, and so on.

For even more of a challenge, make consonant-vowel-consonant (CVC) words with the blocks and then demonstrate how to add the silent *e* at the end to make the vowel sounds long.

Word Families with Blocks

Learning Opportunities

Phonics
Matching

Materials

Square unit blocks
Rectangle unit blocks
Paper
Markers
Tape
Scissors

What to Do

Cut paper into 2 ½-inch squares and 5" x 2 ½" rectangles. Write onsets (the consonant letters or blends at the beginning of words) on the 2 ½-inch squares and rimes (the vowels and letters following the onsets) on the 5" x 2 ½" rectangles. For example, for the rime -*at*, you could add onset blocks with *b-, c-, f-, h-*, and so on. Tape the onsets and rimes to the blocks. Ask the children to put the onsets in front of the rimes to make words.

For a challenge, ask the children to write all the words they can make with a rime; for example, *cot, bot, rot, tot, dot, lot, got, hot,* and *not.*

Sentences with Blocks

Learning Opportunities

Sight words
Sequencing

Materials

Rectangle unit blocks
Paper
Marker
Tape
Scissors

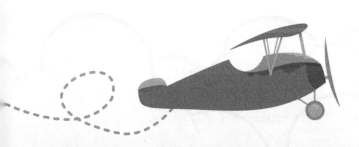

What to Do

Cut paper into 5" x 2 ½" rectangles and write sight words on the rectangles. Challenge the children to put the words together to make sentences that they can read.

For children who need additional support, put *I* on one block and *like* on a second block. Cut out pictures of food and put them on additional blocks. Encourage children to make sentences they can easily read by adding foods to the words *I* and *like*.

Stories and Themes

You can also use blocks with words on them to help children to remember stories and past events and create new stories and settings.

Re-Creating Folktales with Blocks

Learning Opportunities

Recall
Oral language
Creativity
Comprehension

Materials

Blocks
Props such as small toy animals and people

What to Do

Place toys and other props in the block center so the children can retell stories. For example, put toy bears in the block center after reading *Goldilocks and the Three Bears* and encourage the children to build the bears' house. They can also use the blocks to build Jack's beanstalk or a bridge for the three billy goats.

For even more fun, challenge the children to build a castle after reading a fairy tale.

Favorite Characters

Learning Opportunities

Oral language
Imagination
Creativity

Materials

Blocks
Paper-towel tubes cut in half
Pictures of book characters or children's heroes
Tape
Scissors

What to Do

Copy or print pictures of book characters or other children's heroes. Cut out the figures and tape them to the paper-towel tubes so they can stand up. Encourage the children to use their imaginations and create new stories with the characters and blocks.

Re-Creating a Field Trip

Learning Opportunities

Imagination
Creativity
Recall
Engineering skills

Materials

Blocks
Toy farm animals

What to Do

Relate blocks to recent field trips. For example, ask the children to use the toy farm animals and blocks to build a farm after you have visited a local farm.

For even more fun, when studying different habitats, encourage the children to build those habitats with blocks. Provide the children with small toy animals and ask them to make vegetation and other props out of playdough.

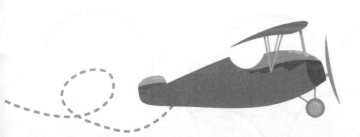

Around the World

Learning Opportunities

Imagination
Creativity
Engineering skills

Materials

Blocks
Pictures of different types of homes in your community and from around the world
Construction paper
Glue
Hole punch
Book rings

What to Do

Print and then cut out pictures of different homes in your city as well as homes from other parts of the world. Glue these to construction paper, punch holes in the papers, and bind them with book rings to make a book. Invite the children to choose homes from the book and try to replicate them with the blocks.

Sensory Explorations Center

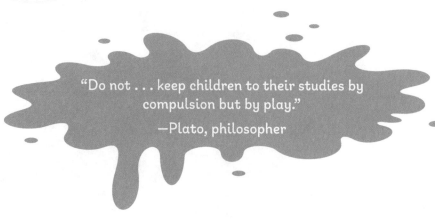

"Do not . . . keep children to their studies by compulsion but by play."

—Plato, philosopher

Children need to explore the physical nature of their world. They need to act on materials—smushing, squeezing, poking, moving, shredding, pouring, sculpting, pushing, pulling, stretching, and tearing as they learn about the properties of materials and the nature of cause and effect (Kemple, 2017). Sand, water, and other "messy" materials give children sensory pleasure while developing their social, language, and small-motor skills and their understanding of math and science concepts.

Materials for the Sensory Explorations Center

Sand or water table (you can also use your classroom sink, plastic tubs, or a wading pool)

Smocks

Towels

Spoons, shovels

Pails

Watering can

Pots, pans, toy dishes

Plastic containers

Plastic bottles

Measuring cups

Funnels

Sponges

Washable baby dolls, clothes

Sifter, strainer

Plastic boats

Ping-Pong balls

Water wheel

Plastic cars and trucks

Plastic animals and toys

Eggbeaters

Eyedroppers

Tip: Ask the children to wash their hands before and after using sensory materials. Model how to clean up messes with sponges, towels, a small vacuum, and so on.

Touching Tub

Learning Opportunities

Sensory exploration
Small-motor skills
Social skills

Materials

Paper confetti
Cotton balls
Water beads
Kinetic sand
Tub

What to Do

Fill the tub with one of these materials. Rotate frequently to keep the children interested in exploring the touching tub. From time to time, talk with a child about the texture of the material she is exploring. Introduce vocabulary, such as *squishy*, *soft*, *gritty*, *slippery*, and so on.

Outside, fill the touching tub with natural objects such as leaves, pine needles, twigs, dirt, and so on. You can also add birdseed so that the birds have a little snack on the playground.

Shave On

Learning Opportunities

Sensory exploration
Small-motor skills

Materials

Non-menthol and non-gel shaving cream
Tub

What to Do

Squirt shaving cream in the tub and invite the children to explore. They can use it like fingerpaint and draw shapes and designs. Encourage the children to practice writing letters, numbers, and their names in the shaving cream.

Outside, children will enjoy exploring with shaving cream on a plastic surface on the playground.

Scoop and Tell

Learning Opportunities

Eye-hand coordination
Small-motor skills
Letter recognition
Shape recognition
Number recognition

Materials

Tub of water
Ping-Pong balls
Permanent marker
Small fishing net, tongs, or large spoons

What to Do

Use a permanent marker to draw letters, shapes, and numerals on Ping-Pong balls, and place them in the water. Invite the children to use a small fishing net, tongs, or large spoons to scoop them up and identify the letters, shapes, or numbers. On a sunny day, take this activity outside.

For a greater challenge, write words or math facts on Ping-Pong balls. Ask the children to identify letters, read the words, or solve the math problems as they fish out the balls.

Bubble Wrap

Learning Opportunities

Sensory exploration
Small-motor skills

Materials

Bubble wrap (large and small bubbles)
Tub or cardboard box

What to Do

Put the bubble wrap with small bubbles in a tub or box, and let the children pop the bubbles with their fingers.

Outside, place the bubble wrap with large bubbles on the pavement so the children can stomp on it and pop the bubbles with their feet.

Icebergs

Learning Opportunities

Observing
Predicting
Vocabulary

Materials

Plastic tub
Plastic containers
Blue food coloring
Plastic Arctic animals

What to Do

Fill the plastic containers with water and add a few drops of food coloring to each. Freeze to make icebergs. Place the icebergs in a tub with the plastic Arctic animals, and encourage the children to play with the animals and observe the melting "icebergs." Ask the children to predict which iceberg will melt the fastest. As they explore, introduce vocabulary such as *freeze, slushy, icy, polar bear, Arctic fox, Arctic wolf, seal, snowy owl, walrus, orca, narwhal,* and so on.

For outside fun, give each child a cup with an ice cube, and challenge them to see who can make their ice cube melt the fastest.

Stretchy Putty

Learning Opportunities

Sensory exploration
Observing
Small-muscle strength

Materials

Craft glue
Liquid starch
Bowl
Spoon
Food coloring
Container with a lid

What to Do

Put 1 cup of glue in the bowl and slowly stir in the starch with a spoon. Knead with your hands. Add more glue or starch until the Stretchy Putty is the desired consistency. Add food coloring and knead. Invite the children to use their hands to stretch and pull the Stretchy Putty. When they are done with this activity, store the Stretchy Putty in a covered container so it does not dry out.

For even more fun, knead glitter into the Stretchy Putty.

Gloop

Learning Opportunities

Exploring
Observing
Tactile experience

Materials

Cornstarch
Water
Food coloring
Bowl
Spoon

What to Do

You will need approximately two parts cornstarch to one part water. Add food coloring to the water. Put the cornstarch in the bowl and slowly stir in the colored water until it reaches the desired consistency. Encourage the children to use their hands to explore the gloop. Introduce vocabulary such as *goopy*, *slippery*, *smooth*, and so on.

For even more fun, offer the children spoons, cups, and other utensils to use with the gloop.

Bubble Machine

Learning Opportunities

Experimenting
Observing

Materials

Tub of water
Liquid dish detergent
Eggbeaters, whisks, basters, and so on

What to Do

Put water in the tub and add a few squirts of dish detergent. Encourage the children to use the eggbeaters, whisks, and other tools to make bubbles.

On a warm summer day, take the bubble machine outside. Ask the children to wear their bathing suits and play in the bubbles. A run through a sprinkler afterwards will ensure that they are clean!

Squeeze Bags

Learning Opportunities

Sensory awareness
Small-motor strength
Exploring
Oral skills
Color recognition

Materials

Ziplock sandwich bags
Shaving cream (non-gel)
Food coloring (red, blue, and yellow)
Packing tape

What to Do

Squirt shaving cream into three bags. Add a drop of red food coloring and a drop of blue food coloring into one bag. Seal with packing tape. Add a drop each of red and yellow food coloring to a second bag, and then seal. Add a drop each of blue and yellow food coloring to a third bag and seal. Put the bags out and observe the children as they squish and squeeze the bags. Encourage them to talk about what happens. Introduce vocabulary such as color names, *squish*, *blend*, *squeeze*, and so on.

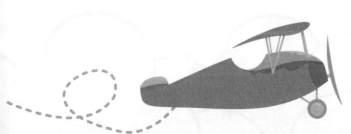

Let's Go to the Beach

Learning Opportunities

Sensory exploration
Experimenting
Observing

Materials

Play sand
Tub
Seashells
Pails
Funnels
Shovels
Paper towel rolls
Other utensils

What to Do

Put several inches of sand in the tub and add a few of the listed materials at a time. Encourage the children to explore and experiment with the funnels, shovels, and so on. For even more fun, add water to the sand so it can be molded.

Dramatic Play Center

> "The world keeps changing, but children
> are the same. They want to be loved, they want to feel
> confident and capable, and they want to play
> and have fun with their friends."
> —Dr. Jean

In the dramatic play area, children role-play real-life situations, release emotions, develop their language and social skills, and express themselves creatively. Use shelves or furniture to create a cozy nook for your dramatic play area. A rug, pictures, and curtains will add a homey feel. Start simply with a basic kitchen set, and slowly add accessories. Label the shelves with pictures and words for where items should be stored. You might consider adding a window to your dramatic play area by attaching an unbreakable mirror or landscape picture to a wall. Tape construction-paper strips to look like a window frame and then add fabric cut like a curtain.

Materials for the Dramatic Play Center

Pretend kitchen equipment made from wood or plastic (stove, refrigerator, sink)

Pots, pans, dishes, utensils

Empty food boxes and containers

Toy food

Dress-up clothes (purses, hats, shoes, jewelry, and so on)

Full-length mirror

Table and chairs

Fabric (for a tablecloth, cape, tent)

Plastic placemats

Multicultural dolls and doll clothes

Stuffed animals (dogs, cats, and so on)

Food dishes for the stuffed animals with cotton balls or other play food

Puppets

Name tags with different characters (mother, father, baby, sister, brother, grandmother, and so on)

Doll bed, blankets

Baby carriage

Toy ironing board and iron

Phones

Old picture frames with children's drawings or class photographs

Car keys

Broom, mop, carpet sweeper

Paper, pencils

Costumes for different careers and ages

Hooks or a hat tree

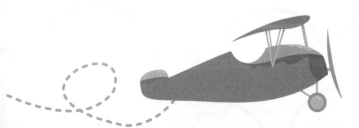

Prop Boxes

Vary the dramatic play area with prop boxes that relate to different themes, units of study, and seasons, or to extend children's interests. Introduce one prop box at a time, and rotate them.

> Tip: Ask a parent volunteer to help collect materials to create different prop boxes.

Birthday Party

Learning Opportunities

Social skills
Oral language
Small-motor skills
Imagination

Materials

Paper
Markers
Party plates, cups, napkins, hats
Favors, goodie bags
Wrapping paper
Tape
Ribbon
Child-safe scissors
Empty boxes
Greeting cards

What to Do

Encourage the children to make invitations for a birthday party and then decorate for it. They can wrap "presents" and set the table for the party. For even more fun, provide party games such as Pin the Tail on the Donkey and a beanbag toss.

Grocery Store

Learning Opportunities

Oral language
Social skills
Imagination
Sorting
Writing numerals

Materials

Empty food boxes and cans*
Grocery sacks
Grocery cart or wagon
Apron
Cash register, play money
Paper and pencils
Purses, billfolds
Sticky dots

*Safety note: Cover sharp edges with duct tape.

What to Do

Ask families to save clean, empty food containers for a week and then bring them into the classroom. Invite the children to help you organize the items on a shelf by different categories (cereal, pasta, tea/coffee, and so on). Help them to put price tags on the items with sticky dots so the children can "shop" and then "purchase" their items.

Post Office

Learning Opportunities

Small-motor skills
Writing skills
Creativity
Self-expression

Materials

Envelopes
Paper
Pencils and pens
Rubber stamps, stamp pad
Stickers
Partitioned box for sorting mail
Bag or sack for carrying mail
Wagon
Box for a mailbox

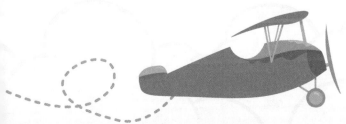

What to Do

Set up a table with paper, pencils, pens, envelopes, rubber stamps and stamp pad, and stickers (pretend postal stamps) where the children can write their letters. Decorate a box with a slit so the children can mail their letters. Children can also use a sack or wagon to deliver the letters to other children and teachers.

For even more fun, plan a field trip to your local post office where children can mail letters they write to their families.

Pet-Supply Store

Learning Opportunities

Oral language
Social skills
Imagination

Materials

Stuffed animals and animal puppets
Cardboard boxes for cages
Plastic bowls
Brush, comb, towel
Cash register, play money
Leashes, collars
Pet toys

What to Do

Invite the children to bring in stuffed animals from home for the pet-supply store. They can shop at the pet store or groom their pets at the grooming station.

For even more fun, add phones and paper so the children can answer calls and fill out forms for grooming appointments.

The Possibilities of Play

Restaurant

Learning Opportunities

Social skills
Self-help skills
Oral language
Imagination
Writing skills

Materials

Paper plates, napkins, plastic cups, and silverware
Tray
Notepad and pencils
Apron
Chef's hat
Menus
Paper and markers
Cash register, play money
Play food
Phone
Unused carry-out food containers, such as pizza boxes

What to Do

Demonstrate to the children how to set a table. Encourage them to take turns setting the table, taking orders, cooking the food, and serving the food. Invite the children to make menus for the restaurant. They can draw pictures and write what they will serve for breakfast, lunch, dinner, and dessert.

If your school has a cafeteria, plan a visit to it for a look "behind the scenes." Ask the cafeteria employees to explain their various tasks to the children.

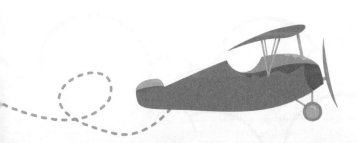

Flower Shop

Learning Opportunities

Oral language
Social skills
Small-motor skills

Materials

Plastic vases
Artificial flowers
Gloves
Seed catalogs
Baskets
Watering can
Play garden tools
Phone
Notepad and pencils
Cash register, play money

What to Do

Encourage the children to take turns taking orders, arranging flowers, and buying and selling items in the flower shop.

For outside fun, let the children "plant" artificial flowers in the sandbox with garden tools.

Doctor's Office/Hospital

Learning Opportunities

Oral language
Social skills
Imagination
Letter recognition

Materials

Stethoscope
Tongue depressors
Cotton
Elastic bandages
Eye chart
Dolls and doll beds
Notepad and pencils
Wagon for ambulance
Phone
Scrub suit and mask

The Possibilities of Play

What to Do

Set up a doctor's office and hospital with doll beds. Invite the children to pretend that they are doctors and/or patients. Post the eye chart and demonstrate how to use it. Encourage the children to take turns reading the eye chart to "check" their eyesight. Show the children how to wrap an ankle or a wrist with an elastic bandage.

For even more fun, invite a doctor or nurse as a guest speaker to talk to the children about how to stay healthy.

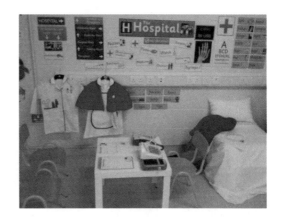

Farmers' Market

Learning Opportunities

Oral language
Social skills
Imagination
Sorting

Materials

Baskets
Plastic fruits and vegetables
Clean, plastic jelly jars
Cash register
Play money and credit cards

What to Do

Ask the children to help you set up the farmers' market by sorting the items into different baskets. Encourage the children to take turns buying and selling the vegetables and fruits.

For even more fun, take a field trip to a local farmers' market.

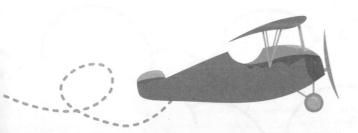

School

Learning Opportunities

Oral language
Social skills
Self-confidence
Imagination
Writing skills

Materials

Desk for teacher
Bell
Calendar
Paper
Crayons, pencils
Books
Eyeglass frames
Chalkboard and chalk or dry-erase board and markers

What to Do

Ask the children to take turns pretending to be the teacher and the students. They will especially enjoy taking the leadership role of the teacher. Encourage the children to use the chalk or markers to "write" homework assignments on the chalkboard or dry-erase board.

For even more fun, change the school center some days by letting the children be the art teacher, music teacher, or physical education teacher. Add relevant items to the prop box.

Hat Shop/Shoe Store

Learning Opportunities

Small-motor skills
Oral language
Social skills
Self-help skills

Materials

Old shoes of different sizes
Hats
Purses
Accessories
Socks
Mirror
Cash register, play money, and credit cards

What to Do

Invite the children to play dress up and try on different shoes, hats, and accessories. They can practice tying shoes and help their friends with this skill as well. Demonstrate pairing together shoes, socks, hats, and accessories, and ask them which items they think work well together.

For even more fun, add dolls so the children can try hats and clothes on the dolls.

Travel Agency

Learning Opportunities

Oral language
Social skills
Imagination
Writing skills

Materials

Travel posters, brochures, pamphlets
Maps
Paper, pencils
Desk, chairs
Phone
Calendar notepad
Souvenirs from other countries
Dress-up clothes

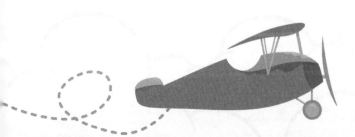

What to Do

Hang up travel posters in a corner of your classroom, and put out brochures, maps, and pamphlets on a table. Demonstrate how a potential traveler would ask questions of a travel agent. Ask the children to make airline, bus, or train tickets for their "customers" (other children).

For even more fun, ask the children to learn about different areas of the world and teach others about their areas.

Ice Cream Shop

Learning Opportunities	Materials
Oral language	Plastic cups, small bowls, spoons
Social skills	Napkins
Imagination	Scoops
Small-motor skills	Empty ice cream cartons
	Pompoms or balls of colored paper for ice cream
	Cash register, play money
	Brown paper
	Tape
	Paper
	Markers

What to Do

Make cones out of brown paper, and set up an ice cream shop so the children can take turns serving the ice cream and buying ice cream cones. Invite the children to create menus for the store by drawing pictures and writing what flavors will be available.

Puppet Theater

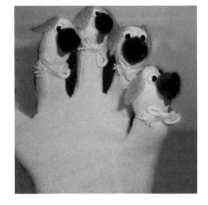

Learning Opportunities

Creativity
Oral language
Social skills

Materials

Large appliance box
Fabric
Glue
Markers
Puppets

What to Do

Turn the box upside down. In the longer side of the box, cut out a large, rectangular hole toward the top to be the stage for the puppet theater. Cut a door in the back of the box so the children can get into it. Glue fabric to the top of the stage for the curtain. Ask the children to decorate the box with markers. Invite them to make a puppet show with the puppets provided. Encourage them to retell familiar stories in the puppet area.

For even more fun, ask the children make their own puppets for their shows. (See pages 187-189 for instructions on how to make different types of puppets.) Some other ideas for puppets include spoon puppets, tube puppets, and glove puppets.

Consider having the children create puppet productions that connect with different themes or holidays. Ask the children to make programs for the show, and invite other classes or families in to watch the show.

My Quiet Place

Learning Opportunities

Self-regulation
Social-emotional skills

Materials

Appliance box
Pillows
Small rug
Stuffed animals
Puppets
Fidget toys

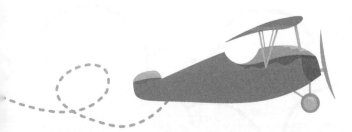

What to Do

Cut the top off the box and put a rug and pillows inside. Add stuffed animals, puppets, fidget toys, and other items children can manipulate with their hands. Knotted socks, chenille stems, Silly Putty, squishy balls, spring-type clothespins, and hair bands are a few examples of items that children can twist, move, and bend to release the wiggles. Place the box in a quiet corner in the classroom, and encourage the children to go there if they need a moment to calm themselves.

For children who need to use fidgets more frequently, make stress buttons. Glue a 1-inch piece of Velcro to a poker chip with strong glue (such as E6000). Allow a child to keep a stress button in his pocket and rub it when his hands are wiggly.

CHAPTER

11

Art Center

When you set up an open art center in your classroom, you invite children to express their creativity in their own unique ways. They will explore materials, such as paint, glue, playdough, and paper, as they imagine and discover the possibilities of these media. They'll also be using engineering skills as they design their inventions and technology skills as they use tools (child-safe scissors, brushes, glue, and so on). They'll be able to make choices, experiment, solve problems, and be truly creative. You can support their explorations by asking them questions to further their thinking (Craft, McConnon, and Matthews, 2012). It's important to provide a wide variety of materials that children can get out easily and clean up independently. To facilitate this, store materials in clear containers and label with words and pictures of the objects.

Remember that it's the process and not the product that matters.

Materials for the Art Center

Shelves to hold materials

Clear containers

Easel

Tables and chairs

Drying rack, smocks

Brushes

Tempera paint

Watercolors

Fingerpaint

Hole punch

Paper (scrap, construction, cardboard, newspaper, tissue paper)

Child-safe scissors

Crayons, colored pencils, markers

Lunch sacks, paper plates

Paper cups

Glue, glue sticks

Material scraps, buttons, yarn

Stapler, tape

Junk scraps (paper-towel tubes, recycled envelopes)

Magazines, catalogs

Chalk

Paper clips, brads

Clay, playdough

Craft sticks

Chenille stems

Natural objects (flowers, leaves, rocks, shells)

Tip: Set up your classroom's art center on a washable floor and near a sink.

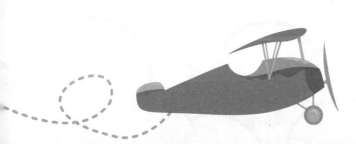

Alphabet Art

Learning Opportunities

Letter recognition
Creativity

Materials

Crayons
Marker
Paper

What to Do

Draw a large letter in the middle of each sheet of paper. Ask each child to choose a letter and then turn the paper all around. Ask them what object, animal, person, or place it looks like. Encourage the children to use crayons to "camouflage" the letters to make them look like something else. Talk about what the word *camouflage* means: "to hide or disguise."

For children who need additional support, draw geometric shapes that children can turn into objects.

For an extra challenge, invite the children to create an object out of the letter that begins with that sound. For example, they could make a house out of the letter *H*.

For even more fun, tie in this activity with particular units of study or seasonal themes. For example, ask the children to make something out of a shamrock on St. Patrick's Day.

The Possibilities of Play

Complete the Picture

Learning Opportunities

Creativity
Visual matching
Small-motor skills

Materials

Crayons
Paper
Glue
Old magazines or catalogs
Scissors

What to Do

Cut out pictures of large objects from magazines. Next, cut the objects in half. Glue one-half of each picture to the left-hand side of a sheet of paper. Ask the children to try to complete the pictures by coloring the missing halves with crayons.

For additional support, cut simple shapes (circle, flower, star, pumpkin, and so on) out of construction paper. Cut the shapes in half and glue one-half of the object to the left-hand side of a sheet of paper. Ask the children to draw and color in the missing half.

Squish Painting

Learning Opportunities

Creativity
Experimenting
Small-motor skills

Materials

Tempera paint
Water
Cups
Paper
Eyedroppers or spoons

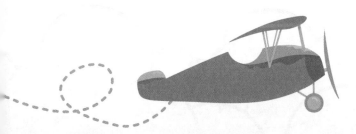

What to Do

Dilute the paint and pour it into cups. Fold sheets of paper in half. Demonstrate to the children how to drop several colors of paint on the paper with the eyedroppers or spoons. Fold the paper in half and rub to make the colors "squish" together. Encourage the children to experiment with this on their own.

For a greater challenge, have the children use primary colors (red, yellow, blue) and name the secondary colors that they create.

For even more fun, cut large butterfly shapes out of paper and use this technique to decorate the butterflies' wings.

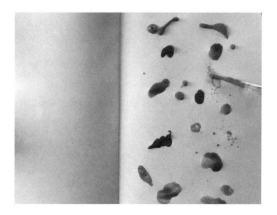 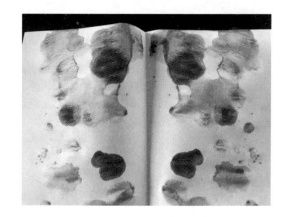

Junk Painting

Learning Opportunities

Experimenting
Creativity

Materials

Spools, kitchen utensils, and other "junk" with interesting textures
Tempera paint
Paper plates
Paper

What to Do

Pour a little paint on the paper plates. Encourage the children to dip the spools, kitchen utensils and other "junk" in the paint and make prints on the paper. Challenge the children to identify the objects that made the different designs.

For outside fun, bring large sheets of newsprint and toy dinosaurs or other plastic animals to the playground. Invite the children to dip the feet of the toys in the paint and let them "walk" across the papers.

Little to Large

Learning Opportunities

Small-motor skills
Spatial awareness

Materials

Crayons
Markers
Paper

What to Do

Make a very small shape or object with a marker in the center of each piece of paper. Give a paper to each child. Ask the children to use a different color of crayon each time and trace around the objects, making them a little larger with each tracing. Encourage them to continue using different colors of crayons and making the objects or shapes a little larger until they completely fill the pages. Consider using seasonal objects (hearts, kites, leaves, and so on) for this activity at another time.

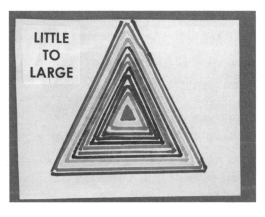

For children who need additional support, draw a small geometric shape on the page to help them learn how to make lines and curves.

Marble Painting

Learning Opportunities

Experimenting
Observing
Small-motor skills

Materials

Marbles
Cups
Tempera paint
Spoons
Paper
Shoeboxes
Scissors
Large cardboard box
Newsprint

What to Do

Cut paper to fit in the bottom of each shoebox. Invite the children to drop marbles in the cups of paint. They can then remove the marbles with spoons and place them in the boxes. Encourage them to tilt the boxes, rolling the marbles around to make designs. If you use two primary colors of paint, the children can observe how they blend to make a secondary color.

For even more fun, roll paper and place it inside an empty oatmeal container or similar cylinder. Ask the children to drop jingle bells in paint and then spoon them into the container. Put on the lid and shake. Remove paper to see the jingle-bell painting.

For outside fun, take a large cardboard box on the playground and put a sheet of newsprint on the bottom. Ask two children to hold the box as you drop in marbles dipped in paint. Encourage them to work together to roll the marbles to decorate the paper.

Negative Space

Learning Opportunities

Creativity
Imagination
Spatial awareness
Small-motor skills

Materials

Crayons
Markers
Scissors
Paper

What to Do

Cut a hole out of the middle of each sheet of paper. (Each hole should be a random shape, about 3 inches in diameter.) Ask each child to choose a sheet of paper and then draw a picture incorporating the hole (negative space). Invite the children to think of titles for their pictures.

Nature Prints

Learning Opportunities

Observing
Creativity
Small-motor skills

Materials

Tempera paint
Paper plates
Large sheets of newsprint
Natural objects such as pine boughs, feathers, sticks, and so on

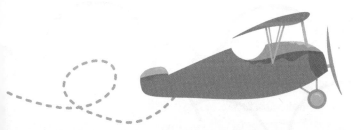

What to Do

Pour a little paint on the paper plates. Invite the children to dip natural objects in the paint and then brush them on their papers.

For extra support, demonstrate how to press items firmly on paper to make a print.

For outside fun, take the paints and paper to the playground and let the children find their own natural objects to print. After the prints dry, see if they can identify the items on their papers.

Torn-Paper Collage

Learning Opportunities

Small-motor skills
Creativity
Imagination

Materials

Scrap paper
Glue
Construction paper

What to Do

Encourage the children to use their fingers to tear scrap paper into little pieces. Ask them to glue the little pieces to larger sheets of paper to make designs or pictures.

For an extra challenge, ask the children to glue the torn paper into geometric shapes, flowers, clouds, and other objects.

For even more fun, cut paper into seasonal shapes, such as flowers or leaves. Have the children tear paper that reflects the seasonal colors. Then, let them glue the torn paper to the shapes and add details with crayons or markers.

Painting with Cotton Swabs

Learning Opportunities

Small-motor skills
Creativity

Materials

Cotton swabs
Tempera paint
Paper
Cups

What to Do

Put a small amount of paint in the cups. Invite the children to dip the ends of cotton swabs in the paint and use as brushes to paint on paper.

For even more fun, mix food coloring with a small amount of water in a cup. Ask the children to paint with the cotton swabs on paper towels. They can also create "invisible paintings" by dipping cotton swabs in water and painting on paper towels.

Rubbings

Learning Opportunities

Small-motor skills
Visual discrimination

Materials

Old crayons
Paper
Textured objects (coins, leaves, sandpaper, comb, and so on)

What to Do

Ask the children to help you tear the outer paper from crayons. Then, invite the children to place paper over the textured objects and rub with the sides of crayons in one direction to make the images appear.

For more fun, challenge the children to make rubbings of puzzles and other school objects.

Outside, encourage the children to make nature rubbings on the playground of tree bark, rocks, flowers, and so on.

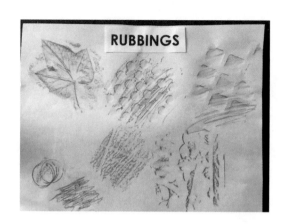

Sponge Prints

Learning Opportunities

Shape recognition
Small-motor strength
Creativity

Materials

Sponges
Scissors
Tempera paint
Paper plates
Paper

What to Do

Cut sponges into geometric shapes. Pour a small amount of paint on each paper plate. Encourage the children to dip the sponges in the paint and press them on paper.

For extra support, offer children a sponge ball or dish mop, which is easier for little hands to press on the paper.

For even more fun, cut sponges into seasonal shapes and use seasonal colors for paint. You can also coordinate sponge prints to units of study. For example, cut sponge airplanes, boats, cars, and trains when doing a transportation theme.

Wheel Painting

Learning Opportunities

Creativity
Exploring
Small-motor skills

Materials

Toy cars, trucks, and other vehicles with wheels
Tempera paint
Large sheets of paper
Paper plates

What to Do

Put a small amount of paint on the paper plates. Ask the children to dip the wheels of the vehicles in the paint, and then "drive" them across the paper.

Take the fun outside by putting newspaper on a paved surface or picnic table so the children have a larger area on which to drive their cars and trucks.

Crayon Bundles

Learning Opportunities

Exploring
Creativity
Small-muscle strength

Materials

Crayons
Rubber bands
Large sheets of paper

What to Do

Wrap rubber bands around sets of three or four crayons to make bundles. Ask the children to hold the bundles in their fists and experiment with making designs on the paper.

For outside fun, put butcher paper on a paved surface or picnic table and encourage the children to use crayon bundles to cover the space. Use the paper for the background on a bulletin board.

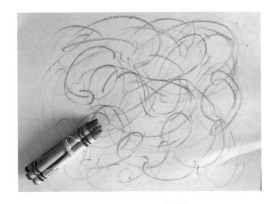

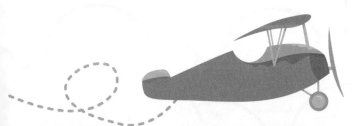

Collage

Learning Opportunities

Using recyclable materials
Creativity
Small-motor skills

Materials

Old catalogs and magazines
Scraps (paper, yarn, fabric, and so on)
Child-safe scissors
Glue
Paper plates

What to Do

Set out old catalogs and magazines as well as junk scraps. Invite the children to cut out pictures from the old catalogs and magazines. Encourage them to glue the cut-out pictures and junk scraps to paper plates to make designs.

Outside, ask the children to collect natural objects such as leaves, flowers, feathers, and so on and to glue them to paper plates to make nature collages. Remind them to collect things off the ground and not pull leaves or flowers off of trees and bushes.

For even more fun, to celebrate Earth Day, give children sentence strips and let them make "nature crowns" by gluing natural objects to the sentence strips. Adjust to their heads and staple or tape the ends together.

Crayon Resist

Learning Opportunities

Experimenting
Observing
Small-motor skills

Materials

Paper
White crayons
Watercolors
Paintbrushes

What to Do

Give each child a white crayon to use to scribble a design on the paper. Next, ask him to use a paintbrush to "wash" over the paper with a watercolor. Encourage children to explain what happens.

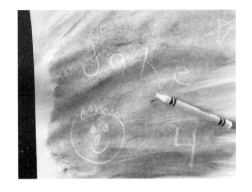

You can also write letters, shapes, or numerals on the paper with a white crayon. Invite each child to choose a paper and then paint over it with the watercolor and identify what is revealed.

For a greater challenge, invite the children to write their names, sight words, or sentences on the papers with white crayons, and then paint over them with a watercolor.

Paper Bag Puppets

Learning Opportunities

Oral language
Imagination
Creativity

Materials

Paper lunch bags
Markers, crayons
Scrap paper
Glue
Child-safe scissors
Buttons, yarn, and other art supplies

What to Do

After reading a favorite book or folktale, ask the children to name their favorite characters. Explain that they can each make a puppet of that character from a lunch bag. Give each child a bag and have her put her hand in it so she knows where the head, mouth, and body should be. Encourage the children to make a plan before creating their puppets. Offer them markers, crayons, scrap paper, scissors, and other materials to make their puppets. Let them collaborate with friends to create a puppet show.

For even more fun, hold a "puppet show and tell" where children describe their puppets to classmates.

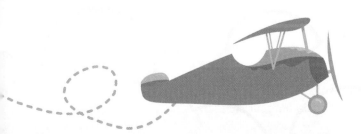

Stick Puppets

Learning Opportunities

Creativity
Oral language
Imagination
Small-motor skills

Materials

Construction paper scraps
Markers, crayons
Child-safe scissors
Craft sticks
Tape

What to Do

Ask the children to draw favorite animals or people on construction paper and decorate with markers and crayons. They can then cut out the figures and tape them to craft sticks.

For children who need extra support, give them outlines of animals and people to choose from to decorate and turn into puppets.

For a greater challenge, divide the children into small groups. Let them plan a puppet show and choose who will make the different puppets. After making their puppets, give them time to practice before presenting the puppet show to their classmates.

For even more fun, invite the children to cut out pictures of people they admire from old magazines, newspapers, and catalogs and then tape the pictures to straws. Ask the children to explain why they admire those people, using their puppets.

Envelope Puppets

Learning Opportunities

Small-motor skills
Creativity
Oral language

Materials

Letter-sized envelopes
Markers, crayons
Buttons, yarn, and other art supplies
Scissors
Glue

What to Do

Seal the envelopes and then cut them in half vertically. Give each child one-half of an envelope and demonstrate how to fit it over their fingers to make a puppet.

Put out markers, crayons, buttons, yarn, and other art supplies. Before getting started, remind the children to think about what they want their puppet to look like. They might want to think of their favorite nursery rhyme and make the main character. They can then take turns using their puppets as they say the rhyme. They can also make farm-animal puppets and use them to sing "The Farmer in the Dell" and other tunes.

For even more fun, ask the children to make puppets for a story you have read. They can use their puppets to "talk" and retell the story.

For a challenge, encourage each child to make a puppet of a hero or someone she'd like to be when she grows up. Each child can use the puppet to explain why she admires that person.

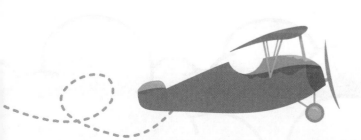

CHAPTER

12

Library
Center

"Play is an important vehicle for developing self-regulation as well as for promoting language, cognition, and social competence."

—*Developmentally Appropriate Practice in Early Childhood Programs Serving Children from Birth through Age 8*, National Association for the Education of Young Children (NAEYC)

The library center should be inviting and interesting because you want the children to fall in love with books. Literacy skills are predictors of children's later achievement (Lonigan, Schatschneider, and Westberg, 2008). In the library area, children develop their oral language, listening, and reading-readiness skills as they explore new concepts. They learn how to hold books, that letters represent sounds, that words have meaning, that the words are read from left to right, and that the pictures show events and characters that are in the text. Put the library in a quiet, cozy corner in the classroom. Carpeting or a rug will keep it warm and inviting.

The Possibilities of Play

Materials for the Library Center

Books in a variety of sizes and shapes

Books on a variety of cultures and subjects, both fiction and nonfiction

Picture books

Sensory books

Flannel board and stories

Comfortable seating (pillows, beanbag chairs, small rocking chair)

Bookrack and shelves

Magazines

Travel brochures

Puppets

Maps

Menus

Dictionary

Pictures and posters

Class-made books

Cool Pool

Learning Opportunities

Motivation to read
Social skills

Materials

Plastic wading pool
Pillows
Stuffed animals
Books

What to Do

Put pillows, stuffed animals, and books in the plastic pool. Encourage the children to relax and explore the books. Consider limiting the number of children in the pool to minimize behavior issues.

For even more fun, on a rainy day, open a large golf umbrella and put books under it. Children can snuggle up with a friend and share a good book.

Reading Clubhouse

Learning Opportunities

Motivation to read
Social skills
Oral language
Imagination

Materials

Large appliance box
Craft knife (Adult use only)
Scissors
Poster board
Paint
Paintbrushes
Markers
Flashlight or child-safe lantern

What to Do

Use the craft knife to cut a window and door in the appliance box to make a reading clubhouse. Make a sign that says, "Readers Only" and add it to the front of the box. Let children brainstorm how they'd like to decorate their reading clubhouse, and then provide them with paints, markers, and paintbrushes. Cut poster board into 2" x 3" rectangles and invite the children make their individual "membership cards" for the club. (Of course, every child gets a membership card!)

Put books and the flashlight or lantern in the reading clubhouse and encourage a few children at a time to read inside.

For even more reading fun, make a reading tent by placing a blanket over a table. Store books in a backpack under the table and add a flashlight.

Mirror, Mirror

Learning Opportunities

Motivation to read
Oral language
Self-confidence

Materials

Full-length mirror
Books

What to Do

Hang a full-length mirror at children's eye level in the library center. Encourage the children to choose a book and then "read" it in the mirror.

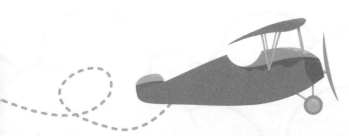

For even more fun, add twinkle lights, seasonal objects, and other novelty items that will spark children's interest in visiting the library center.

Author Study

Learning Opportunities

Motivation to read
Oral language
Asking questions

Materials

Basket or tub
Books by a favorite author
Author's photo

What to Do

After introducing a children's author and reading several books by that author, put the books in a basket, attach the author's photo to the basket, and place it in your library center. Tell the children a little about the author and invite them to ask questions.

For even more fun, ask the children to vote on their favorite book by an author.

For a greater challenge, encourage the children to draw pictures and write letters to a favorite author.

Read to a Star

Learning Opportunities

Motivation to read
Oral language

Materials

Photos of popular athletes, movie stars, authors, and musicians
Clear sheet protectors or plastic picture frames

What to Do

Place the pictures in clear sheet protectors or picture frames and add them to your library center. Ask each child to choose a person and then "read" to that person.

For even more fun, put action figures and other toys in the library to use as reading buddies.

For a greater challenge, provide the children with paper, pencils, and crayons so they can draw pictures and write letters to the "stars."

Flannel Board

Learning Opportunities

Oral language
Comprehension
Small-motor skills

Materials

File folder or unused pizza box
Felt
Craft glue
Scissors
Stapler
Velcro
Pictures of superheroes, animals, community helpers, and so on

What to Do

To make a flannel board, staple two open sides of a file folder to make a pocket, and glue felt to the front. Alternatively, you can use a clean pizza box and glue felt to the inside of the lid. Cut small strips of Velcro (hook side) and glue them to the backs of the pictures. Store the pictures inside the file folder or pizza box. Invite the children to take out the characters and use them to make up stories.

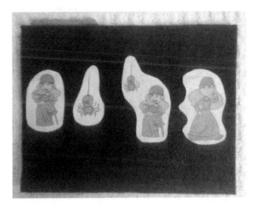

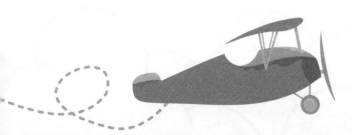

For even more fun, make characters for traditional folktales, such as Goldilocks and the Three Bears, the Little Red Hen and her friends, Anansi the Spider, and Fox and the Gingerbread Boy, and encourage the children to use the characters to retell the folktales.

Bookmarks

Learning Opportunities

Motivation to read
Small-motor skills

Materials

Construction paper
Yarn
Markers
Glue
Scissors

What to Do

Cut heart shapes out of the construction paper. Cut the yarn into 7-inch pieces. Show the children how to fold the hearts in half. Then, ask them to open the hearts, put glue on one side, insert the strip of yarn, and press to seal. Invite the children to decorate the folded hearts to look like mice or other animals. Show them how to insert the tail in the page they want to save when reading a book and then close the book.

Pointers, Pointers

Pointers support children in advancing their reading skills by helping them focus, track left to right, and develop eye-hand coordination when they look at books and other reading materials.

Keep Your "Eye" on the Words

Learning Opportunities

Eye-hand coordination

Left-to-right orientation

Materials

Jumbo craft sticks
Googly eyes
Craft glue

What to Do

Glue googly eyes to the ends of craft sticks. Encourage the children to use these to "keep their eyes on the words" as they read. They can use their eye sticks to point to and focus on details in illustrations, find words that they can read, and identify punctuation.

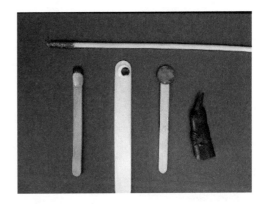

Finger Pointer

Learning Opportunities

Eye-hand coordination
Left-to-right orientation
Letter recognition

Materials

Craft sticks
Fake fingernails
Craft glue

What to Do

Glue fake fingernails to the ends of craft sticks. Encourage the children use these fingernail pointers to track print in books, find letters in their names, and notice other details.

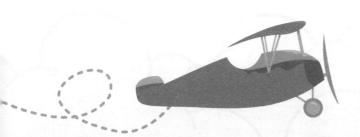

Magic Wand Pointer

Learning Opportunities

Eye-hand coordination
Left-to-right orientation
Letter recognition

Materials

Chopsticks
Glue
Glitter

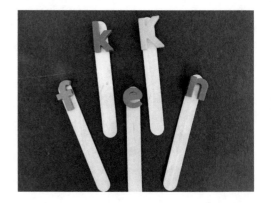

What to Do

Roll the ends of chopsticks in glue and then dip them in glitter. Allow the glue to dry. Invite the children to use their magic wands to point to letters and pictures as they read books in the library center.

Letter Pops

Learning Opportunities

Eye-hand coordination
Left-to-right orientation
Letter recognition

Materials

Magnetic letters
Jumbo craft sticks
Craft glue
Can

What to Do

Make a letter pop by gluing a magnetic letter to one end of a jumbo craft stick. Keep these letter pops in a can in the classroom library. Ask each child to pick a letter pop and then find that letter in a book.

The Possibilities of Play

CHAPTER

13

Listening & Technology Center

Computers, tablets, and other interactive devices are a common part of our everyday lives and can be used to enhance and enrich young children's learning environment. When implemented in intentional and developmentally appropriate ways, technology is an effective tool for supporting children's learning (NAEYC and the Fred Rogers Center for Early Learning and Children's Media at Saint Vincent College, 2012).

Listening Center

The listening center enables children to follow along as they hear books being read. They can make connections with illustrations, print, and words.

Materials for the Listening Center

Tablets	Pointers
Headphones	Paper
Recordings of songs	Pencils
Books	Crayons

Activities for the Listening Center

We've included a variety of learning songs, seasonal songs, and silly songs that children will enjoy hearing over and over.

"Alligator Chant" https://www.youtube.com/watch?v=yJiTWd-250A

"Alphabet Forwards and Backwards" https://www.youtube.com/watch?v=VC_DhG3bTxA

"Banana Dance" https://www.youtube.com/watch?v=MFmr_TZLpS0

"Be a Buddy" https://www.youtube.com/watch?v=EQaWZZnFww0

"Chant and Write" https://www.youtube.com/watch?v=J0WOnslkjXI

"Days of the Week" https://www.youtube.com/watch?v=oKqAblcwFOA

"Dinosaur Boogie" https://www.youtube.com/watch?v=kS1cPJhQPmM

"Cool Bear Hunt" https://www.youtube.com/watch?v=1P__9XSPYkk

"Katalina Matalina" https://www.youtube.com/watch?v=20vNvMdz7BU

"Mother Goony Bird" https://www.youtube.com/watch?v=9—zaOSh8Tc

"Over in the Meadow" https://www.youtube.com/watch?v=gvWGWLUZiZU

"Pizza Hut" https://www.youtube.com/watch?v=teprteZCKV8

"Phon-ercise" https://www.youtube.com/watch?v=OxrUgwVbqoM

"Rise and Shine" https://www.youtube.com/watch?v=JljSW1cuYsc

"Rules Rap" https://www.youtube.com/watch?v=z60vA7vVYUY

"The Alphabet in My Mouth" https://www.youtube.com/watch?v=UyHypl9Cdr0

"The Color Farm" https://www.youtube.com/watch?v=LlgZjl_K8vA

"Today Is Sunday" https://www.youtube.com/watch?v=-JsfKTNAL50

"Weather Song" https://www.youtube.com/watch?v=wDyGRf8ChYc

"Wiggle Willy" https://www.youtube.com/watch?v=wYd6UJt8uGE

Technology Center

Children can use computers to read, write, illustrate, practice math facts, watch science videos, and so on. The opportunities for learning are endless.

Materials for the Technology Center

Computers

Tablets

Headphones

Paper

Pencils

Digital camera

Interactive whiteboard

Boom box or mp3 player

Coding set, such as Botley, Cubelets, or Bee-Bot

The Possibilities of Play

Pick and Type

Learning Opportunities

Visual matching
Keyboarding

Materials

Sand bucket
Index cards
Permanent marker
Computer

What to Do

Write letters on the index cards and place them in the sand bucket. Ask a child to choose a letter and then type it on the computer. You can also repeat this activity with numerals.

For a greater challenge, write children's names on the index cards and ask them to type their names on the computer.

K Computer

Learning Opportunities

Interest in technology
Keyboarding
Visual matching

Materials

Pocket folder
Keyboard pattern
Glue
Index cards
Marker

What to Do

Glue the keyboard pattern to the inside of the pocket folder. On the index cards, write the children's names, letters, and so on, and place them in the pocket. Ask the children to choose a card and then match and "type" the letters on the keyboard pattern.

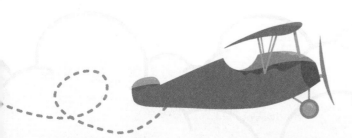

Picture Treasure Hunt

Learning Opportunities

Identifying shapes, colors, or beginning letter sounds
Creativity
Cooperation

Materials

Tablet

What to Do

Choose a treasure-hunt topic for the day, such as a color, shape, or beginning letter sound. Ask the children to work in pairs to hunt for objects in the classroom to go with the topic. When they find something, ask them to take a picture of it with a tablet. After center time, encourage the pairs to share the "treasures" they collected on their tablets with the rest of the class.

Take the fun outside and hold an outdoor treasure hunt where children can collect pictures of leaves, clouds, flowers, bugs, things that start with a particular sound, and so on.

Interviews

Learning Opportunities

Oral language skills
Self-confidence
Communication

Materials

Tablet

What to Do

Choose an interview question for each child to answer and then record a video of each child's interview. Ask the children to give reasons for their answers. Some possible questions include the following:

- What is your favorite animal? Why?
- What is your favorite food for dinner?
- What is your favorite game to play? Whom do you play it with?
- What is your favorite thing to do at school?
- What is your favorite candy?
- What is your favorite fruit?

- What is your favorite vegetable?
- What is your favorite book?
- Do you have any pets? If yes, what kind? If no, what kind of pet would you like to have?
- Do you have any brothers or sisters?
- Do you like summer or winter better? Why?
- What do you do before bed?
- What do you do before school?

When you've completed the interviews, have a celebration as you share the interview videos with the class.

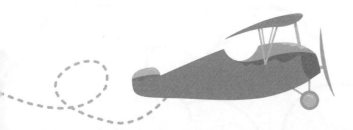

CHAPTER

14

Outdoor Adventures

> "Children of all ages love to play, and it gives them opportunities to develop physical competence and enjoyment of the outdoors, understand and make sense of their world, interact with others, express and control emotions, develop their symbolic and problem-solving abilities, and practice emerging skills."
>
> —*Developmentally Appropriate Practice,*
> NAEYC

Outside is one of the healthiest and happiest places for children to grow and develop. They develop their physical, social, emotional, language, and cognitive skills on the playground and in outdoor spaces. Children who spend time in nature experience less stress and better concentration, are more active and creative, and are better able to interact positively with others (Taylor and Kuo, 2006). Outdoor experiences also provide children with lots of opportunities for developing math and science understanding. If possible, consider planting a garden in your outdoor space. The children will enjoy planting, watering, and observing the plants that grow there, as well as discovering the creatures that visit the garden.

Materials for Outdoor Adventures

Sandbox

Shovels, buckets

Water

Cups, sieves, ladles

Riding toys

Wagon

Climbing equipment

Swings

Slide

Balls (all sizes)

Paved surface

Grassy area

Water table

Smocks

Bird feeder

Outdoor kitchen

Traffic signs, such as stop, yield, speed limit, and pedestrian crossing signs

Digging for Worms

Learning Opportunities

Sensory exploration

Oral-language skills

Small-motor skills

Materials

Potting soil

Earthworms (real or fake)

Plastic tweezers

Shovels, spoons, scoops

Tub

Magnifying glasses

Paper towels

What to Do

Put the potting soil in the tub and add the worms. Ask the children to use their fingers or tweezers to remove the worms from the tub and place them on paper towels for observation. If you're using real earthworms, talk with the children about being gentle and returning the worms to the soil after they have studied them for a few minutes. Talk with the children about how earthworms help the soil.

Mud Pies

Learning Opportunities

Sensory exploration
Small-motor skills
Imagination
Oral-language skills

Materials

Soil
Water
Bowls or buckets
Spoons

What to Do

Show the children how to mix equal parts soil and water and slowly stir to get the desired consistency. Encourage the children to mold mud into mud pies and other objects. They can decorate their creations with sticks, leaves, and flowers and let them dry in the sun.

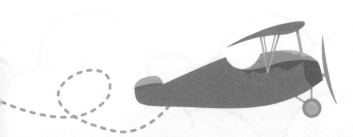

Snow Fun

Learning Opportunities

Sensory exploration
Observing
Small-motor strength

Materials

Snow, shaved ice, or artificial snow
Empty spray bottles
Food coloring
Water
Bucket
Tub
Containers and molds

What to Do

This is a fun activity to do if you live in an area that receives lots of snow. But if a snowy day is unlikely in your area, you can use shaved ice or artificial snow, such as Miracle Snow. Add a few drops of food coloring to spray bottles filled with water. Encourage the children to squirt the colored water on the snow and observe what happens. Invite the children to play with the snow and observe as it melts. They can also fill containers and mold the snow.

Rock and Wash

Learning Opportunities

Sensory exploration
Small-motor strength

Materials

Rocks
Vegetable scrub brushes
Old toothbrushes
Sponges
Dish detergent
Tub

What to Do

Let the children collect rocks on the playground—the dirtier the better. Fill a tub with water and dish detergent. Ask the children to scrub the rocks with the brushes and sponges.

For even more fun, invite the children to paint the rocks and use them to make a rock garden on the playground.

Gold Diggers

Learning Opportunities

Sensory exploration
Imagination
Communication skills

Materials

Small rocks or pebbles
Gold spray paint
Sifters
Sandbox

What to Do

Away from the children, spray-paint rocks and pebbles gold to make "nuggets." Hide the gold pebbles in the sandbox. Provide the children with sifters, and encourage them to use the sifters to hunt for "gold" in the sand. For even more fun, let the children take turns hiding and finding them.

Magnets

Learning Opportunities

Observing
Experimenting

Materials

Sandbox
Metallic objects (paper clips, metal toys, jar lids, binder clips, and so on)
Magnets

What to Do

Hide metallic objects in the sandbox. Give the children magnets and ask them to use the magnets to find the objects.

For even more fun, hide magnetic letters in the sand for the children to find and identify.

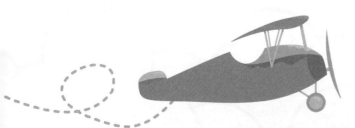

Sink and Float

Learning Opportunities

Predicting
Sorting
Experimenting

Materials

Tub of water
Objects that will sink (plastic toys, metal spoon, pennies, marbles, rubber balls, blocks, and so on)
Objects that will float (leaves, paper, craft sticks, rubber ducky, boat, plastic food, and so on)

What to Do

Place the objects next to the tub of water. Ask the children to sort the objects by predicting which ones will sink and which ones will float. Ask them why they think some of the objects will sink or float. Then, encourage them to experiment by putting the objects in the water to see if their predictions are correct. Ask them to think about how the objects that float are alike and how the objects that sink are alike.

For even more fun, ask the children to find natural objects (sticks, leaves, rocks, and so on) on the playground and predict which ones will sink and float.

Bath Time

Learning Opportunities

Sensory exploration
Self-help skills

Materials

Tub of soapy water
Plastic baby dolls
Washcloths
Sponges
Towels

What to Do

Fill the tub half full with soapy water. Encourage the children to wash the baby dolls in the tub and then dry them off.

For even more fun, tie a string between two trees to make a clothesline. Let the children wash the doll clothes and then hang them up on the clothesline to dry.

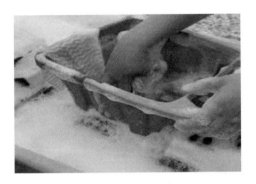

Boats Afloat

Learning Opportunities

Engineering skills
Experimenting
Observing

Materials

Tub of water
Aluminum foil
Craft sticks
Paper bowls

What to Do

Put out the materials and then challenge the children to design and build boats that will float. After they have made their boats and tested them in the water, ask the children which design worked best.

Box Blocks

Learning Opportunities

Large-motor skills
Engineering skills
Social skills

Materials

Large cardboard boxes
Packing or duct tape

What to Do

Ask families to save large cardboard boxes and send them to school. Tape the boxes shut and then take them out on the playground. Ask the children to stack the boxes and create structures with them.

For even more fun, invite the children to paint the boxes.

Reading Tent

Learning Opportunities

Motivation to read
Oral language

Materials

Blanket or sheet
Basket
Books
Beach towel

What to Do

Place books in the basket. Invite the children to help you construct a tent by draping the blanket or sheet over a picnic table or card table. Place a beach towel on the floor of the tent. Encourage the children to choose books from the basket and enjoy sharing books with their friends.

Notetakers

Learning Opportunities

Prewriting skills
Observing
Creativity

Materials

Clipboards
Paper
Pencils

What to Do

Encourage the children to become notetakers on the playground. Offer them clipboards on which they can draw pictures of what they see. Consider offering this activity every season so that children can observe the seasonal changes.

For a greater challenge, invite the children to write or draw stories and poems while they are outside.

For children who need support, they can dictate what they want to write as you record it for them. You can help them write some of the letters in the words.

Campsite

Learning Opportunities

Learning about nature
Social skills
Engineering skills

Materials

Rocks
Sticks
Blankets and sheets
Rope

What to Do

Invite the children to share any camping experiences. Ask, "How do you build a tent?" Discuss different ways to build tents and let them experiment with the blankets and sheets. They may decide, for example, to drape a blanket over a picnic table. They may wish to tie a rope to a tree and drape a blanket or sheet over it.

Ask, "How do you build a campfire?" Facilitate a discussion on why you put rocks around the outside of a campfire, and put sticks in the middle. Encourage the children to use the rocks and sticks to construct a "campfire."

For a greater challenge, sit around the campfire and sing camp songs such as "Found a Peanut," "Home on the Range," and "100 Bottles of Pop on the Wall."

Cardboard Castle

Learning Opportunities

Creativity
Social skills
Small-motor skills

Materials

Large appliance box
Utility knife (Adult use only)
Paints
Paintbrushes

What to Do

With the utility knife, cut a door and some windows out of the box. Encourage the children to decorate the box with paint to make it a castle for pretend play.

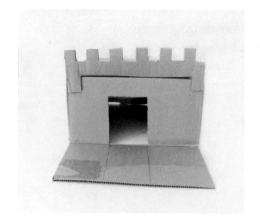

Fence Art

Learning Opportunities

Creativity
Social skills
Experimenting
Patterns

Materials

Large plastic cups (different colors)
Chain-link fence

What to Do

Demonstrate how to insert the bottom of a plastic cup into a hole in the chain-link fence. Let the children experiment with the cups to get them to stay in the fence. Ask the children to make shapes with the cups in the fence. Can they make a pattern with the cups? When they are finished exploring, you can recycle the cups.

For a greater challenge, divide the children into small groups and ask them to decorate the fence for a school celebration or holiday.

Water Painting

Learning Opportunities

Creativity
Exploring
Observing
Small-motor skills

Materials

Sand pails or plastic containers
Paintbrushes
Water

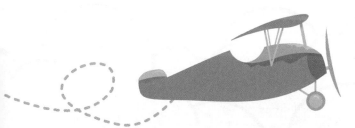

What to Do

Fill the plastic sand pails or containers with water and give the children paintbrushes. Tell them they can paint the school building, windows, playground equipment, sidewalk, trees, or anything they want. Ask them to observe what happens to the water when it dries. Where does it go?

For even more fun, offer the children different sizes of paintbrushes, sponges, wash rags, and so on. You can also squirt shaving cream on the classroom windows and let the children fingerpaint. Cleanup is easy with a water hose.

Sidewalk Artists

Learning Opportunities

Creativity
Small-motor skills
Social skills

Materials

Colored chalk
Box
Paved surface

What to Do

Put the colored chalk in a box and place it on the paved surface so the children can freely explore drawing on pavement with chalk.

Reinforce skills you are working on in the classroom by asking the children to write letters, numbers, their names, and so on.

For even more fun, invite the children to decorate the sidewalk for special school events and holidays.

Dirt Painting

Learning Opportunities

Creativity
Exploring
Small-motor skills

Materials

Water
Dirt
Plastic containers
Paintbrushes
Paper

What to Do

Mix the dirt with water to make a thick liquid in plastic containers. Offer the children paintbrushes and encourage them to paint dirt pictures with the paintbrushes or with their fingers on paper.

For even more fun, look for different types of soil to create different shades of "dirt" paint that children can paint with.

Fence Painting

Learning Opportunities

Creativity
Small-motor skills

Materials

Large sheets of paper
Spring-type clothespins
Paints
Paintbrushes
Fence

What to Do

Attach large sheets of paper to a fence with the clothespins. Offer the children paint and paintbrushes, and encourage them to paint the large sheets of paper.

For even more fun, put the paint in pie pans and give the children clean fly swatters to dip in the paint and swat on the paper.

Fitness Trail

Learning Opportunities

Large-motor skills
Following directions
Recognizing numerals

Materials

Poster board or cardboard
Markers
Clear sheet protectors
Tape

What to Do

Involve the children in creating a fitness trail for the playground. Cut the poster board or cardboard into 8 ½" x 11" sheets. Number each of the sheets with a numeral from 1 to 10 and write a different activity on each one. Include fitness activities such as:

Do ten jumping jacks

Say a nursery rhyme

Do eight windmills

Count to ten

Do twelve squats

Name five insects

Run in place

Hop on one foot, hop on the other foot

Sing the ABCs

Do fifteen toe touches

Laminate or put the signs in clear sheet protectors so they can be used for several weeks. Hang the activities around the playground at appropriate spots, and invite the children to follow the fitness trail.

For children who need extra support, make the activities simpler by asking children to say their full name, jump five times, sing a song, tiptoe, and so on.

For an extra challenge, include activities that have the children count backwards from 20 to 1; name their city, state, and country; skip; and so on.

Driver's Ed

Learning Opportunities

Large-motor skills
Following directions
Spatial awareness
Writing skills

Materials

Chalk
Riding toys
Cardboard
Glue
Scissors
Children's photos
Markers

What to Do

Cut the cardboard into 3 ¼" x 2 ¼" rectangles. Create a "road test" by drawing arrows on a sidewalk with chalk. In the road test, children must ride toys on a straight line, stop, turn around, and so on.

Explain to the children what to do and let them practice. After passing the test, ask the children to make their driver's licenses. They can glue their photos to the cardboard rectangles and then write their names.

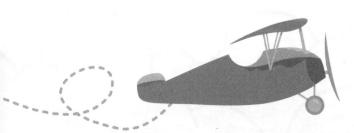

References and Recommended Reading

Almon, Joan, and Edward Miller. 2011. "The Crisis in Early Education: A Research-Based Case for More Play and Less Pressure." *Alliance for Childhood* http://www.teachingwithlove.com/Case%20for%20recess/ The%20Crisis%20in%20Early%20Education.pdf

Barbour, Ann. 2016. *Play Today: Building the Young Brain through Creative Expression.* Lewisville, NC: Gryphon House.

Bodrova, Elena, Carrie Germeroth, and Deborah Leong. 2013. "Play and Self-Regulation: Lessons from Vygotsky." *American Journal of Play* 6(1): 111–123.

Broadhead, Pat, Justine Howard, and Elizabeth Wood, eds. 2010. *Play and Learning in the Early Years: From Research to Practice.* London, UK: SAGE.

Brown, Stuart. 2008. "Play Is More than Just Fun." TED video. https://www.ted.com/talks/stuart_brown_play_ is_more_than_just_fun?language=en#t-16388

Brown, Stuart, and Christopher Vaughan. 2010. *Play: How it Shapes the Brain, Opens the Imagination, and Invigorates the Soul.* New York: Penguin.

Byington, Teresa, and YaeBin Kim. 2017. "Promoting Preschoolers' Emergent Writing." *Young Children* 72(5): 74–82.

Carlson, Frances. 2011. "Rough Play: One of the Most Challenging Behaviors." *Young Children* 66(4): 18–25.

Clements, Douglas, and Julie Sarama. 2014. *Learning and Teaching Early Math: The Learning Trajectories Approach.* 2nd ed. New York: Routledge.

Copple, Carol, and Sue Bredekamp, eds. 2009. *Developmentally Appropriate Practice in Early Childhood Programs Serving Children from Birth through Age 8.* Washington, DC: NAEYC.

Craft, Anna, Linda McConnon, and Alice Matthews. 2012. "Child-Initiated Play and Professional Creativity: Enabling Four-Year-Olds' Possibility Thinking." *Thinking Skills and Creativity* 7(1): 48–61.

Dewar, Gwen. 2014. "The Cognitive Benefits of Play: Effects on the Learning Brain." Parenting Science. https:// www.parentingscience.com/benefits-of-play.html

Erikson, Erik. 1950/1963. *Childhood and Society.* New York: W. W. Norton.

Fisher, Kelly, et al. 2013. "Taking Shape: Supporting Preschoolers' Acquisition of Geometric Knowledge through Guided Play." *Child Development* 84(6): 1872–1878.

Gerde, Hope, Gary Bingham, and Barbara Wasik. 2012. "Writing in Early Childhood Classrooms: Guidance for Best Practices." *Early Childhood Education Journal* 40(6): 351–359.

Ginsberg, Herbert, and Kyoung-Hye Seo, 2009. "Mathematics in Children's Thinking." *Mathematical Thinking and Learning* 1(2): 113–129.

Ginsburg, Kenneth R., Committee on Communications, and Committee on Psychosocial Aspects of Child and Family Health. 2007. "The Importance of Play in Promoting Healthy Child Development and Maintaining Strong Parent-Child Bonds." *Pediatrics* 119(1): 182–191.

Grissmer, David, et al. 2010. "Fine Motor Skills and Early Comprehension of the World: Two New School Readiness Indicators." *Developmental Psychology* 46(5): 1008–1017.

Hanline, Mary Frances, Sande Milton, and Pamela Phelps. 2001. "Young Children's Block Construction Activities: Findings from 3 Years of Observation." *Journal of Early Intervention* 24(3): 224–237.

Hirsh-Pasek, Kathy, and Roberta M. Golinkoff. 2003. *Einstein Never Used Flash Cards: How Our Children Really Learn—and Why They Need to Play More and Memorize Less*. Emmaus, PA: Rodale.

Hook, Pamela, and Sandra Jones. 2004. "The Importance of Automaticity and Fluency for Efficient Reading Comprehension." *Perspectives on Language and Literacy* 30 (Spring): 16–21.

Kemple, Kristen. 2017. *Planning for Play: Strategies for Guiding Preschool Learning*. Lewisville, NC: Gryphon House.

Kostelnik, Marjorie, et al. 2014. *Developmentally Appropriate Curriculum: Best Practices in Early Childhood Education*. 6th ed. Boston, MA: Pearson.

Levine, Susan, et al. 2011. "Early Puzzle Play: A Predictor of Preschoolers' Spatial Transformation Skill." *Developmental Psychology* 48(2): 530–542.

Lonigan, Christopher, Chris Schatschneider, and Laura Westberg. 2008. "Identification of Children's Skills and Abilities Linked to Later Outcomes in Reading, Writing, and Spelling." *Developing Early Literacy: Report of the National Early Literacy Panel*. Louisville, KY: National Center for Family Literacy.

Mayer, Kelley. 2007. "Emerging Knowledge about Emergent Writing." *Young Children* 62(1): 34–41.

Miller, Edward, and Joan Almon. 2009. *Crisis in the Kindergarten: Why Children Need to Play in School*. College Park, MD: Alliance for Childhood.

NAEYC and the Fred Rogers Center for Early Learning and Children's Media at Saint Vincent College. 2012. *Technology and Interactive Media as Tools in Early Childhood Programs Serving Children from Birth through Age 8*. Washington, DC: NAEYC.

National Council for the Social Studies. 2010. *National Curriculum Standards for Social Studies: A Framework for Teaching, Learning, and Assessment.* Washington, DC: National Council for the Social Studies.

The National Institute for Play. n.d. "The Science: Pattern of Play." The National Institute for Play.

Nayfield, Irena, Rochel Gelman, and Kimberly Brenneman. 2011. "Science in the Classroom: Finding a Balance Between Autonomous Exploration and Teacher-Led Instruction in Preschool Settings." *Early Education and Development* 22(6): 970–988.

Neumann, Michelle, Michelle Hood, and Ruth Ford. 2012. "Using Environmental Print to Enhance Emergent Literacy and Print Motivation." *Reading and Writing* 26(5): 771–793.

Nicolopoulou, Ageliki. 2010. "The Alarming Disappearance of Play from Early Childhood Education." *Human Development* 53(1): 1–4.

Parten, Mildred B. 1932. "Social Participation among Pre-School Children." *The Journal of Abnormal and Social Psychology* 27(3): 243–269.

Quinn, Margaret, Hope Gerde, and Gary Bingham. 2016. "Help Me Where I Am: Scaffolding Writing in Preschool Classrooms." *The Reading Teacher* 70(3): 353–357.

Ratey, John. 2008. *Spark: The Revolutionary New Science of Exercise and the Brain.* New York: Little, Brown.

Raver, Cybele. 2002. "Emotions Matter: Making the Case for the Role of Young Children's Emotional Development for Early School Readiness." *Social Policy Report of the Society for Research in Child Development* 16(3): 1–20.

Rowe, Deborah, and Carin Neitzel. 2010. "Interest and Agency in 2- and 3-Year-Olds' Participation in Emergent Writing." *Reading Research Quarterly* 45(2): 169–195.

Rymanowicz, Kylie. 2015. "The Power of Play—Part 1: Stages of Play." Michigan State University Extension, October 6. https://www.canr.msu.edu/news/the_power_of_play_part_1_stages_of_play

Shonkoff, Jack P., and Deborah A. Phillips. 2000. *From Neurons to Neighborhoods: The Science of Early Child Development.* Washington, DC: National Academies Press.

Singer, Dorothy, Roberta Golinkoff, and Kathy Hirsh-Pasek. 2006. *Play=Learning: How Play Motivates and Enhances Children's Cognitive and Social-Emotional Growth.* New York: Oxford University Press.

Sutherland, Shelbie L., and Ori Friedman. 2013. "Just Pretending Can Be Really Learning: Children Use Pretend Play as a Source for Acquiring Generic Knowledge." *Developmental Psychology* 49(9): 1660–1668.

The Possibilities of Play

Taylor, Andrea, and Frances Kuo. 2006. "Is Contact with Nature Important for Healthy Child Development? State of the Evidence." In *Children and Their Environments: Learning, Using, and Designing Spaces.* Cambridge, UK: Cambridge University Press.

Taylor, Andrea, and Frances Kuo. 2009. "Children with Attention Deficits Concentrate Better after a Walk in the Park." *Journal of Attention Disorders* 12(5): 402–409.

Wang, Sam, and Sandra Aamodt. 2012. "Play, Stress, and the Learning Brain." *Cerebrum* Sept-Oct. https://www.dana.org/article/play-stress-and-the-learning-brain/

Weisberg, Deena, et al. 2015. "Making Play Work for Education: Research Demonstrates that Guided Play Can Help Preschool Children Prepare for Reading and Math Better than Free Play and Direct Instruction Alone." *Phi Delta Kappan* 96(8): 8–13.

Wolfgang, Charles H., Laura L. Stannard, and Ithel Jones. 2001. "Block Play Performance among Preschoolers as a Predictor of Later School Achievement in Mathematics." *Journal of Research in Childhood Education* 15(2): 173–180.

Zigler, Edward, Dorothy Singer, and Sandra Bishop-Josef, eds. 2004. *Children's Play: The Roots of Reading.* Washington, DC: Zero to Three.

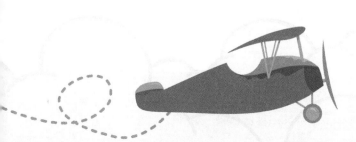

Index

A

Addition
  block center, 142
  math center, 101–102
Alphabet knowledge
  literacy center, 44
  small-motor center, 34
  writing center, 79
Alphabet recognition
  listening center, 203–204
  literacy center, 61
  writing center, 76
American Sign Language, 61
Art center, 2, 13, 18, 173–189
  collages, 182, 186
  color recognition, 178–179
  creativity, 174, 176–179, 181–189
  engineering skills, 174
  experimenting, 174, 177–180, 186–187
  exploring, 185
  imaginative and pretend play, 181–182, 187–188
  letter recognition, 176
  making choices, 174
  materials, 175
  observation skills, 180–182, 186–187
  oral language skills, 187–189
  problem-solving skills, 174
  recall, 188–189
  shape recognition, 184
  small-motor skills, 177–189
  spatial awareness, 179, 181
  storytelling-narrative play, 188–189
  technology skills, 174
  using recyclable materials, 186
  visual matching, 177
Asking questions, 117, 196
Attention span, 22
Automaticity, 12

B

Balance, 9
Beginning letter sounds, 206
Bilateral coordination, 23
Blank books, 79–86
Block center, 2, 8, 13, 18, 131–150
  addition, 142
  building math concepts, 139–142
  comprehension skills, 148
  counting skills, 140–141
  creativity, 134, 136–138, 148–150
  engineering skills, 134, 136–137, 149–150
  environmental print, 137
  eye-hand coordination, 136, 138–139
  imaginative and pretend play, 132, 149–150
  letter recognition, 143–145
  literacy skills, 143–150
  matching, 143–144, 146–147
  materials, 133
  math skills, 139–142
  name recognition, 144–145
  number recognition, 132, 140–142
  oral language skills, 132, 138, 144, 146, 149
  phonics, 143, 146–147
  recall, 148–149
  rhyming, 144
  rules, 132
  self-confidence, 132
  self-help skills, 139–140
  sight words, 144–145, 147–148
  small-motor skills, 134–138
  social/emotional skills, 132, 138–139
  sorting skills, 139–140
  spatial awareness, 134–136
  storytelling-narrative play, 145
  upper- and lowercase letters, 143
  visual discrimination, 183–184
  visual matching, 139–140
  visual skills, 134–135

Body play and movement, 5–7
Book-handling skills
    library center, 192
    writing center, 80–81, 83, 85

C

Cardinality, 95–96
Cause and effect, 153
Choice board, 13–14
Choices, 9, 174
Classifying, 113, 117
Cognitive development
    outdoor play, 209
    play and, 7–8
Collages
    art center, 182, 186
    small-motor center, 23
Color recognition
    art center, 178–179
    literacy center, 48
    science center, 114–116
    sensory explorations center, 157
    small-motor center, 22, 40
    technology center, 206
Color words, 62
Communication skills, 6, 12
    outdoor play, 213
    science center, 114–115
    technology center, 206–207
Comparing skills
    math center, 88, 102–104
    science center, 119
    small-motor center, 39
Comprehension skills
    block center, 148
    library center, 197
    small-motor center, 35
    writing center, 81
Cooperation skills, 6, 12
    science center, 114
    technology center, 206
Counting skills
    block center, 140–141

math center, 88, 90–91, 94, 97–98, 102–103, 107–108
    science center, 116, 126–127
Creativity
    art center, 174, 176–179, 181–189
    block center, 134, 136–138, 148–150
    dramatic play center, 163–164, 171
    outdoor play, 216, 218–221
    science center, 124–125
    small-motor center, 23, 25, 32, 40
    technology center, 206
    writing center, 80
Critical-thinking skills, 12

D

Decision-making skills, 110
Discovery bottles, 118–125
Dramatic play center, 1, 18, 159–172
    adding writing materials, 67
    creativity, 163–164, 171
    imaginative and pretend play, 162–170
    letter recognition, 166–167
    materials, 161
    oral language skills, 160, 162–171
    prop boxes, 162–172
    self-confidence, 168
    self-expression, 163–164
    self-help skills, 165, 169
    self-regulations skills, 171–172
    small-motor skills, 162–164, 166, 169–170
    social/emotional skills, 160, 162–172
    sorting skills, 163, 167
    writing numerals, 163
    writing skills, 163–165, 168–170

E

Emergent spelling, 46
Emergent writing skills
    science center, 116
    small-motor center, 35–36
    writing center, 71–73
Engineering skills
    art center, 174
    block center, 134, 136–137, 149–150

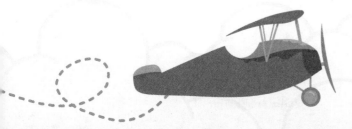

outdoor play, 215–218

small-motor center, 40

Environmental print

    block center, 137

    literacy center, 44, 53–54

    writing center, 81

Estimating, 96, 102

Executive function skills, 6, 12

Experimenting

    art center, 174, 177–180, 186–187

    outdoor play, 213, 215, 219

    science center, 114–116, 118–124

    sensory explorations center, 156–158

Exploring

    art center, 185

    outdoor play, 219–221

    sensory explorations center, 156–157

Eye-hand coordination

    block center, 136, 138–139

    library center, 198–200

    math center, 104–105

    sensory explorations center, 154

    small-motor center, 22–26, 28, 30, 37, 40

    writing center, 71

F

Following directions, 222–223

G

Guided play, 8

H

Homemade playdough, 33–34

Home-school connection, 80

Hygiene, 22, 32, 153

I

Imaginative and pretend play, 5

    art center, 181–182, 187–188

    block center, 132, 149–150

    dramatic play center, 162–170

    library center, 194–195

    outdoor play, 211, 213

science center, 111–113

science center, 124

small-motor center, 32

Independence, 7, 23, 25, 30, 32

Independent exploration, 18

Intentional teaching, 9

J

Joining in play, 7

Journals, 15

L

Large-motor skills

    math center, 99

    outdoor play, 216, 222–223

Learning about nature, 216–218

Learning centers, 1, 9

    art, 2, 13, 18, 173–189

    block, 2, 8, 13, 18, 131–150

    checklist, 14

    choice board, 14

    clothespins, bracelets, and badges, 17

    dramatic play, 1, 18, 159–172

    journals, 15

    library, 2, 13, 18, 191–200

    listening, 2, 18, 201–204

    literacy, 2, 43–63

    managing, 11–19

    materials management, 19

    math, 2, 18, 87–108

    outdoor play, 2, 6, 9, 208–223

    pick three, 16

    rotation, 18

    science, 2, 18, 109–129

    sensory explorations, 2, 13, 152–158

    small-motor, 2, 21–42

    task cards, 15

    technology, 2, 18, 201, 214–207

    tickets to, 16

    tips for success, 13

    writing, 2, 65–85

Left-to-right orientation

    library center, 192, 198–200

literacy center, 51
writing center, 73–74
Letter recognition
art center, 176
block center, 143–145
dramatic play center, 166–167
library center, 199–200
literacy center, 45–50, 52–54, 57
math center, 99
sensory explorations center, 154
small-motor center, 27, 34–36
writing center, 67–68, 75–78, 80–85
Library center, 2, 13, 18, 191–200
asking questions, 196
book-handling skills, 192
comprehension skills, 197
eye-hand coordination, 198–200
imaginative and pretend play, 194–195
left-to-right orientation, 51, 192, 198–200
letter recognition, 199–200
listening skills, 192
literacy skills, 192
materials, 193
motivation to read, 194–198
oral language skills, 192, 194–197
phonics, 48, 54–56, 59–60, 192
reading-readiness skills, 192
self-confidence, 195–196
small-motor skills, 197–198
social/emotional skills, 194–195
Listening center, 2, 18, 201–204
alphabet recognition, 203–204
materials, 202
singing, 202–204
Listening skills, 6, 192
Literacy center, 2, 43–63
alphabet knowledge, 44
alphabet recognition, 61
color recognition, 58
color words, 62
emergent spelling, 46
environmental print, 44, 53–54
letter recognition, 45–50, 52–54, 67

materials, 45
name recognition, 50–52, 55
oral language skills, 44–45
phonological awareness, 44–45
print knowledge, 45, 50–52, 62
rhyming, 56, 59–60
sight words, 48, 52, 54, 57
small-motor skills, 52, 59, 61
storytelling-narrative play, 45
tracking print, 62–63
upper- and lowercase letters, 48, 54–56, 59–60
visual discriminations, 53, 60, 62
visual matching, 58, 60, 62
visual memory, 58
writing skills, 45, 47, 57, 60
Literacy skills
block center, 143–150
library center, 192
play and, 8
playdough center, 34–36

M

Making play suggestions, 7
Making sets, 96
Matching, 95, 143–144, 146–147
Math center, 2, 18, 87–108
addition, 101–102
cardinality, 95–96
comparing skills, 88, 102–104
counting skills, 88, 90–91, 94, 97–98, 102–103, 107–108
estimating, 96, 102
eye-hand coordination, 104–105
inequalities, 96
joining and separating sets, 88
large-motor skills, 99
letter recognition, 99
making sets, 96
matching sets and numbers, 95
materials, 89
measuring, 88, 102–104
number recognition, 94, 99–102, 107–108
one-to-one correspondence, 90–91
operations, 90

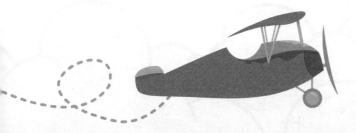

patterns, 88, 90, 92
place value, 107
sensorimotor skills, 106
sequencing skills, 142, 146–148
shape recognition, 88, 104–106
sight words, 99
small-motor skills, 88, 90–93, 97–98, 105, 107–108
sorting skills, 88, 96, 105
subitizing, 93, 100–101
visual discrimination, 96
visual matching, 94
writing numerals, 97–98, 107–108
Measuring
math center, 88, 102–104
science center, 141
Memory, 7, 58, 60, 62–63
Modeling, 13, 88
Motivation to read
library center, 194–198
outdoor play, 216
writing center, 80–85
Motivation to write, 79–85

N

Name recognition
block center, 144–145
literacy center, 50–52, 55
writing center, 81–82
Number recognition
block center, 132, 140–142
math center, 94, 99–102, 107–108
outdoor play, 222–223
sensory explorations center, 154
small-motor center, 38

O

Observation skills
art center, 180–182, 186–187
outdoor play, 212–213, 215–216, 219–220
science center, 113–116, 118–124, 126, 128–129
sensory explorations center, 155–158
small-motor center, 41
One-to-one correspondence

math center, 90–91
small-motor center, 38
Oral language skills
art center, 187–189
block center, 132, 138, 144, 146, 149
dramatic play center, 160, 162–171
library center, 192, 194–197
literacy center, 44–45
outdoor play, 210–211, 216
play and, 7–8
sensory explorations center, 157
small-motor center, 22–23, 35–36
technology center, 206–207
Organizational skills, 12
Outdoor play, 2, 6, 9, 208–223
cognitive development, 209
communication skills, 213
creativity, 216, 218–221
engineering skills, 215–218
experimenting, 213, 215, 219
exploring, 219–221
following directions, 222–223
imaginative and pretend play, 211, 213
large-motor skills, 216, 222–223
learning about nature, 216–218
materials, 210
motivation to read, 216
number recognition, 222–223
observation skills, 212–213, 215–216, 219–220
oral language skills, 210–211, 216
patterns, 219
predicting, 214
prewriting skills, 216
science center, 209
self-help skills, 214–215
sensorimotor skills, 210–215
small-motor skills, 210–212, 218–221
social/emotional skills, 209, 216–220
sorting skills, 214
spatial awareness, 223
writing skills, 223

P

Patterns, 22
>math center, 88, 90, 92
>outdoor play, 219
Persistence, 132
Phonics
>block center, 143, 146–147
>library center, 192
>literacy center, 48, 54–56, 59–60
>technology center, 206
>writing center, 81, 85
Phonological awareness, 18, 44–45
Play, 3–9
>benefits for the whole child, 8–9
>children's right to, 1–2
>cognitive development, 7–8
>physical development, 6–7
>social-emotional development, 6
>stages and types, 4–5
Playdough center, 18, 32–41
>homemade playdough, 33–33
>literacy skills, 34–36
>sight words, 36
>STEM learning, 37–41
Predicting
>outdoor play, 214
>science center, 122, 125–129
>sensory explorations center, 155
>small-motor center, 40
Prewriting skills
>outdoor play, 216
>science center, 123–124, 129
>small-motor center, 28
>writing center, 67–70, 72–73, 75
Print knowledge, 45, 50–52, 62
Problem-solving skills, 6, 12
>art center, 174
>science center, 110
>small-motor center, 32
Prop boxes, 162–172
Puppets, 187–189

R

Reading-readiness skills, 18
>library center, 192
>small-motor skills and, 22
>technology center, 204
Ready to write, 74–79
Recall
>art center, 188–189
>block center, 148–149
>writing center, 85
Recording data, 114, 126–129
Responsibility, 12
Rhyming
>block center, 144
>literacy center, 56, 59–60

S

Scaffolding, 71
Science center, 2, 18, 109–129
>adding writing materials, 67
>asking questions, 117
>classifying, 113, 117
>color recognition, 114–116
>communication skills, 114–115
>comparing skills, 119
>cooperation skills, 114
>counting skills, 116, 126–127
>creativity, 124–125
>decision-making skills, 110
>discovery bottles, 118–125
>emergent writing skills, 116
>experimenting, 114–116, 118–124
>imaginative and pretend play, 111–113, 124
>materials, 111
>measuring, 141
>observation skills, 113–116, 118–124, 126, 128–129
>playing with water, 125–129
>predicting, 122, 125–129
>prewriting skills, 123–124, 129
>problem-solving skills, 110
>recording data, 114, 126–129
>scribbling and drawing, 116
>self-expression, 124

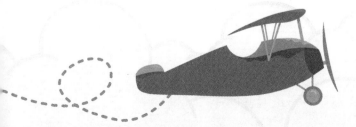

sensorimotor skills, 110

singing, 111–113

small-motor skills, 115–116, 125, 128–129

social/emotional skills, 124

sorting skills, 113, 116–117, 126–127

using recyclable materials, 119–124

vocabulary, 111–113, 126–127

writing skills, 114

Scribbling and drawing, 116

Self-confidence

block center, 132

dramatic play center, 168

library center, 195–196

small-motor center, 30

technology center, 206–207

writing center, 80

Self-expression

dramatic play center, 163–164

science center, 124

small-motor center, 32

Self-help skills, 7

block center, 139–140

dramatic play center, 165, 169

outdoor play, 214–215

small-motor center, 26, 31

Self-regulation skills, 171–172

Sensorimotor skills

math center, 106

outdoor play, 210–215

science center, 110

sensory explorations center, 154–158

writing center, 76-77

Sensory explorations center, 2, 13, 152–158

cause and effect, 153

color recognition, 157

experimenting, 156–158

exploring, 156–157

eye-hand coordination, 154

letter recognition, 154

materials, 153

number recognition, 154

observation skills, 155–158

oral language skills, 157

predicting, 155

sensorimotor skills, 154–158

shape recognition, 154

small-motor skills, 154–157

social/emotional skills, 154

tactile experience, 156

vocabulary, 155

Sequencing skills

math center, 142, 146–148

small-motor center, 35

writing center, 82

Shape recognition

art center, 184

math center, 88, 104–106

sensory explorations center, 154

small-motor center, 22, 27, 37, 39

technology center, 206

writing center, 77, 85

Sight words

block center, 144–145, 147–148

literacy center, 48, 52, 54, 57

math center, 99

playdough center, 36

Singing

listening center, 202–204

science center, 111–113

Small-motor center, 2, 21–41

alphabet knowledge, 34

attention span, 22

bilateral coordination, 23

collages, 23

color recognition, 22, 40

comparing skills, 39

comprehension skills, 35

creativity, 23, 25, 32, 40

emergent writing skills, 35–36

engineering skills, 40

eye-hand coordination, 22–26, 28, 30, 37, 40

imaginative and pretend play, 32

independence, 23, 25, 30, 32

interest in nature, 41

investigation skills, 41

letter recognition, 27, 34–36

The Possibilities of Play

literacy skills, 34
materials for, 22
number recognition, 38
observation skills, 41
one-to-one correspondence, 38
oral language skills, 22–23, 35–36
playdough center, 32–41
predicting, 40
prewriting skills, 28
problem-solving skills, 32
self-confidence, 30
self-expression, 32
self-help skills, 26, 31
sequencing skills, 35
shape recognition, 22, 27, 37, 39
small-motor skills, 21–41
social/emotional skills, 22–23, 32
spatial awareness, 24–25, 30, 39
STEM learning, 37–41
task initiation and completion, 25, 27–28, 34, 37
testing hypothesis, 40
using recyclable materials, 136–137
Small-motor skills
   art center, 177–189
   block center, 134–138
   dramatic play center, 162–164, 166, 169–170
   library center, 197–198
   literacy center, 52, 59, 61
   math center, 88, 90–93, 97–98, 105, 107–108
   outdoor play, 210–212, 218–221
   science center, 115–116, 125, 128–129
   sensory explorations center, 154–157
   small-motor center, 21–41
   technology center, 205
   writing center, 67–78, 80–85
Social/emotional skills
   block center, 132, 138–139
   dramatic play center, 160, 162–172
   library center, 194–195
   outdoor play, 209, 216–220
   play and, 6
   science center, 124
   sensory explorations center, 154

   small-motor center, 22–23, 32
Songs, 202–204
Sorting skills
   block center, 139–140
   dramatic play center, 163, 167
   math center, 88, 96, 105
   outdoor play, 214
   science center, 113, 116–117, 126–127
   writing center, 82
Spatial awareness
   art center, 179, 181
   block center, 134–135
   outdoor play, 223
   small-motor center, 24–25, 30, 39
STEM learning, 37–41
Storytelling-narrative play, 5
   art center, 188–189
   block center, 148
   literacy center, 45
Stress, 6, 32
Subitizing, 93, 100–101

T

Task initiation and completion, 7
   small-motor center, 25, 27–28, 34, 37
   writing center, 73–74
Teacher as facilitator, 12–13
Teacher-directed activities, 18
Technology center, 2, 18, 201, 204–207
   beginning letter sounds, 206
   color recognitions, 206
   communication skills, 206–207
   cooperation skills, 206
   creativity, 206
   interest in technology, 205
   keyboarding skills, 205
   materials, 204
   math skills, 204
   oral language skills, 206–207
   phonics, 206
   reading-readiness skills, 204
   science skills, 204
   self-confidence, 206–207

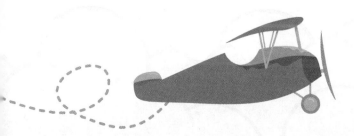

shape recognition, 206
small-motor skills, 205
Tracking print, 62–63

U

Upper- and lowercase letters
 block center, 143
 literacy center, 48, 54–56, 59–60
Using recyclable materials
 art center, 186
 block center, 136–137
 science center, 119–124
 small-motor center, 28, 30

V

Visual discrimination
 art center, 183–184
 block center, 142
 literacy center, 53, 60, 62
 math center, 96
Visual matching
 art center, 177
 block center, 139–140
 literacy center, 58, 60, 62
 math center, 94
 technology center, 205
Visual skills, 134–135
Vocabulary, 7
 science center, 111–113, 126–127
 sensory explorations center, 155
 writing center, 68

W

Water play, 125–129
Writing center, 2, 65–85
 alphabet knowledge, 79
 alphabet recognition, 76
 book-handling skills, 80–81, 83, 85
 comprehension skills, 81
 creativity, 80
 emergent writing skills, 71–73
 emergent writing, 71–73
 environmental print, 81

eye-hand coordination, 71
I'm a writer, I'm an author, 79–85
left to right, 73–74
left-to-right orientation, 73–74
letter recognition, 67–68, 75–78, 80–85
materials, 67
math skills, 79, 81
motivation to read, 80–85
motivation to writing, 79–85
name recognition, 81–82
phonics, 81, 85
prewriting skills, 67–70, 72–73, 75
ready to writing, 74–79
recall, 85
repetition, 72
science skills, 79
self-confidence, 80
sensorimotor skills, 76–77
sequencing skills, 82
shape recognition, 77, 85
small-motor skills, 67–78, 80–85
sorting skills, 82
task initiation and completions, 73–74
themes, 82
vocabulary, 68
Writing numerals, 97–98, 107–108, 163
Writing skills
 dramatic play center, 163–165, 168–170
 literacy center, 45, 47, 57, 60
 outdoor play, 223
 science center, 114
 writing center, 76, 78–85

The Possibilities of Play